# Beyond "Good Night, Moon"

# 75 Reviews of Classic Books For Young Children

*Happy Reading!*

## By Joan Louthain Ayer

*Joan Ayer*

First published by Dog Ear Publishing
4010 W. 86th Street, Ste H
Indianapolis, IN 46268
www.dogearpublishing.net

ISBN: 1-59858-240-2
Library of Congress Control Number:   2006936722

This book is printed on acid-free paper.

Printed in the United States of America

Dedicated to the Memory

of my mom and dad

Lige and Elizabeth Louthain

# Introduction

As a fresh-out-of-college 21 year old in the fall of 1963, I began teaching second grade at the largest elementary school in Madison, Wisconsin. There were more than 1000 students at Frank Allis Elementary, and 34 of them were in my classroom, during an era when teaching aides did not exist.

It didn't take me long to discern that if the students were going to learn anything, classroom control with a modicum of quiet was definitely an issue. Luckily, classroom libraries were common in those days, and I began reading to the children nearly every day. I often read to them after the noon recess, and "Millions of Cats" by Wanda Gag was a popular choice. Quiet prevailed almost instantly whenever I began reading.

Thirty years later when I was teaching preschool in Terre Haute, Indiana, those three and four year olds loved that classic book too. They also loved nearly every other book that I have included in this anthology.

While we were living in Terre Haute, I also did a great deal of substitute teaching, sometimes in fifth or sixth grade classrooms—-not exactly my forte. On one particular occasion in a fifth grade classroom, the movie projector became uncooperative, spoiling the planned lesson for that period. Fortunately, I spotted a copy of "Sarah, Plain and Tall" by Patricia MacLachlan. An overlarge boy, obviously the spokesperson for the group, said "You're going to read to us!" his voice dripping with condescending tones. Needless to say, he and all the others became quiet within about 30 seconds, caught up in MacLachlan's spell. When the period was over they begged for more, even though they were scheduled to move on to a different classroom.

After I had written my newspaper column about children's books for several years, people sometimes spoke to me about their read aloud experiences with their children or other people's children, for that matter. Two well-loved aunts often told me about books they had read to or purchased for their nieces or nephews.

A few young mothers told me that they not only started reading to their infants as soon as they were born, but also read to them in the womb! Tiny babies make a wonderful audience, because they can't get away and love the sound of your voice as you are holding them.

Which leads me to one of the best "reading" stories I ever heard. A young man spoke to me at the grocery store one time and told me that he often read to his two year old stepson from "Car and Driver" magazine! Pausing only briefly I said "Well, that's good" and quietly suggested a few titles that he could find at the library that might be just a little more appropriate.

These stories, then and many, many more are the reason why, I have chosen to write "Beyond Good Night, Moon." The author of that book, Margaret Wise Brown, is actually one of my favorites, but I am partial to her other books such as "Little Fur Family", "Big Red Barn" and "The Runaway Bunny" which have a bit more story to them. "Little Fur Family" is our granddaughter Mary's favorite. She is four now, but she has loved it and "Big Red Barn" since she was about two.

So as young parents, grandparents, special aunties, nannies or teachers of young children, we hope you will comb through this anthology of classic books and find some favorites from your own childhood to share with those special little people in your lives.

Don't let expense become an excuse for you. Many of these books are available as paperbacks, and I've found lots and lots of them, too, at second bookstores, library book sales or even garage sales, sometimes for as little as a dime or a quarter.

Many of these books are also currently available as board books, the perfect size for toddler hands.

All of these books are field-tested, in that I have read them aloud many times to little ones myself.

SATA (Something About the Author) is a series of reference books which contains biographies of children's authors, which I used extensively for this anthology and also while I was writing my newspaper column.

Copyright dates noted with each review are the original copyright dates.

As I write this, a few of these books are currently out of print, but thankfully classics such as these are reissued fairly often.

Finally, we wanted to keep the size of this book small enough so that dads (and moms) could slip it in their briefcase before they head out on a business trip. As we hope you all know, a book beats a battery-operated thing-a-ma-jig every time, when choosing gifts for your precious children.

# Table of Contents

1. Anderson, C. W.—"Billy and Blaze" c. 1936. . . . . . .1

2. Asch, Frank—"Happy Birthday, Moon" c. 1982. . . . .2

3. Bemelmans, Ludwig—"Madeline" c. 1939. . . . . . . .3

4. Beskow, Elsa—"Pelle's New Suit" c. 1929. . . . . . . .4

5. Bornstein, Ruth—"Little Gorilla" c. 1976. . . . . . . . .5

6. Bridwell, Norman—"Clifford, the Small Red Puppy" c. 1972. . . . . . . . . . . . . . . . . . . . . . . . . . . . . . .7

7. Bright, Robert—"Georgie" c. 1944. . . . . . . . . . . . .8

8. Brown, Margaret Wise—"The Runaway Bunny" c. 1942. . . . . . . . . . . . . . . . . . . . . . . . . . . . . . . .9

9. Buckley, Helen E.—"Grandfather and I" c. 1959. . . .10

10. Burton, Virginia Lee—"The Little House" c. 1942 .11

11. Carle, Eric—"The Grouchy Ladybug" c. 1977. . . . .12

12. Carlstrom, Nancy White—"Jesse Bear What Will You Wear?" c. 1986. . . . . . . . . . . . . . . . . . . . . . . . .13

13. Cooney, Barbara—"Miss Rumphius" c. 1978. . . . . .14

14. Crews, Donald—"Freight Train" c. 1978. . . . . . . . .15

15. DePaola, Tomie—"Charlie Needs A Cloak" c. 1973 17

16. DePaola, Tomie—"Pancakes For Breakfast" c. 1978.18

17. Degan, Bruce—"Jamberry" c. 1983. . . . . . . . . . . . .19

18. Dennis, Wesley—"Flip" c. 1941. . . . . . . . . . . . . . .21

19. DeRegniers, Beatrice Schenk—"May I Bring A Friend?" c. 1964. . . . . . . . . . . . . . . . . . . . . . . . . .22

20. Eastman, P.D.—"Are You My Mother?" c. 1960. . . .23

21. Ets, Marie Hall—"Play With Me" c. 1960. . . . . . . .24

22. Flack, Marjorie—"Angus and the Cat" c. 1955. . . . .25

23.  Flack, Marjorie—"Ask Mr. Bear" c. 1932. . . . . . . . .26
24.  Frank, Josette—"Poems to Read to the Very Young"
     c. 1961 . . . . . . . . . . . . . . . . . . . . . . . . . . . . . . .28
25.  Freeman, Don—"Corduroy" c. 1968. . . . . . . . . . . .30
26.  Gag, Wanda—"Millions of Cats" c. 1928. . . . . . . . .31
27.  Galdone, Paul—"The Little Red Hen" c. 1973. . . . .32
28.  Galdone, Paul—"The Teeny Tiny Woman" c. 1984. .34
29.  Graham, Margaret Bloy—"Be Nice to Spiders"
     c. 1967. . . . . . . . . . . . . . . . . . . . . . . . . . . . . . . .35
30.  Gramatky, Hardie—"Little Toot" c. 1939. . . . . . . . .36
31.  Guilfoile, Elizabeth—"Nobody Listens to Andrew"
     c. 1957. . . . . . . . . . . . . . . . . . . . . . . . . . . . . . . .38
32.  Henkes, Keven—"Jessica" c. 1989. . . . . . . . . . . . . .39
33.  Heyward, Du Bose—"The Country Bunny and The
     Little Gold Shoes" c. 1939. . . . . . . . . . . . . . . . . . .40
34.  Hoban, Russell—"Bedtime For Frances" c. 1960, . .41
35.  Hoff, Syd—"Danny and the Dinosaur" c. 1958. . . . .42
36.  Hoff, Syd—"The Littlest Leaguer" c. 1976. . . . . . . .44
37.  Hogrogian, Nanny—"One Fine Day" c. 1971. . . . . .45
38.  Johnson, Crockett—"Harold and the Purple Crayon"
     c. 1955 . . . . . . . . . . . . . . . . . . . . . . . . . . . . . . . .46
39.  Kalan, Robert—"Jump, Frog, Jump" c. 1981. . . . . .47
40.  Keats, Ezra Jack—"The Snowy Day" c. 1962. . . . . .48
41.  Kent, Jack—"The Fat Cat"—a Danish Folk Tale
     c. 1971. . . . . . . . . . . . . . . . . . . . . . . . . . . . . . . .49
42.  Krasilovsky, Phyllis—"The Man Who Didn't Wash His
     Dishes" c. 1950. . . . . . . . . . . . . . . . . . . . . . . . . .51
43.  Krauss, Ruth—"The Carrot Seed" c. 1945. . . . . . . .53
44.  Leaf, Munro—"The Story of Ferdinand" c. 1946. . .54

45. Lionni, Leo—"Frederick" c. 1967. . . . . . . . . . . . . .55

46. Lobel, Arnold—"Frog and Toad Together" c. 1971.  56

47. Lopshire, Robert—"Put Me In the Zoo" c. 1960. . . .57

48. Lowrey, Janet Sebring—"The Poky Little Puppy"
    c. 1942. . . . . . . . . . . . . . . . . . . . . . . . . . . . . . . .58

49. Martin, Bill Jr.—"Brown Bear, Brown Bear, What
    Do You See?" c. 1967. . . . . . . . . . . . . . . . . . . . . . .59

50. Mayer, Mercer—"When I Get Bigger" c. 1983. . . . .60

51. McGovern, Ann—"Too Much Noise" c. 1967. . . . . .62

52. McKloskey, Robert—"Make Way For Ducklings"
    c. 1941. . . . . . . . . . . . . . . . . . . . . . . . . . . . . . . .63

53. Minarik, Else Holmelund—"Little Bear" c. 1957. . .65

54. Munsch, Robert—"Thomas' Snowsuit" c. 1985. . . .66

55. Nodset, Joan—"Who Took the Farmer's Hat?"
    c. 1963. . . . . . . . . . . . . . . . . . . . . . . . . . . . . . . .67

56. Numeroff, Laura Joffe—"If You Give a Mouse a
    Cookie" c. 1985. . . . . . . . . . . . . . . . . . . . . . . . . .69

57. Perkins, Al—"The Diggingest Dog" c. 1967. . . . . . .71

58. Piper, Wally—"The Little Engine That Could"
    c. 1930. . . . . . . . . . . . . . . . . . . . . . . . . . . . . . . .72

59. Potter, Beatrix—"The Tale of Peter Rabbit" c. 1901. 73

60. Rey, H.A. and Margret—"Curious George Goes to
    the Hospital" c. 1966. . . . . . . . . . . . . . . . . . . . . . .74

61. Sendak, Maurice—"Pierre, a Cautionary Tale"
    c. 1962. . . . . . . . . . . . . . . . . . . . . . . . . . . . . . . .76

62. Seuss, Dr.—"Green Eggs and Ham" c. 1962. . . . . . .78

63. Slobodkina, Esphyr—"Caps For Sale" c. 1940. . . . .80

64. Steig, William—"Doctor De Soto" c. 1982. . . . . . . .81

65. Stone, Jon—"The Monster at the End of The Book"
    c. 1971. . . . . . . . . . . . . . . . . . . . . . . . . . . . . . . .82

66. Tresselt, Alvin—"The Mitten" c. 1964. . . . . . . . . . .84

67. Udry, Janice May—"A Tree Is Nice" c. 1956. . . . . .85

68. Viorst, Judith—"Alexander, Who Used to Be Rich Last Sunday" c. 1978. . . . . . . . . . . . . . . . . . . . . . . . . . . .87

69. Waddell, Martin—"Owl Babies" c. 1975. . . . . . . . .88

70. Wood, Audrey—"The Napping House" c. 1984. . . .90

71. Zion, Gene—"Harry, the Dirty Dog" c. 1958. . . . . .91

72. Zion, Gene—"No Roses For Harry" c. 1958. . . . . . .93

73. Zolotow, Charlotte—"I Like to Be Little" c. 1987. .95

74. Zolotow, Charlotte—"Mr. Rabbit and the Lovely Present" c. 1962. . . . . . . . . . . . . . . . . . . . . . . . . . . . . .96

75. Zolotow, Charlotte—"William's Doll" c. 1972. . . . .97

# 1. Billy & Blaze   Story and pictures by C. W. Anderson c.1936

Luckily for all of us, Clarence Wilson Anderson lived to be 80 years old. This enabled him to write and illustrate more than 35 horse stories before his death in 1971. None have endured like his Billy & Blaze stories for children. He renewed the copyright himself in 1964, and the sepia-colored Aladdin paperbacks became available for just $3.95 in 1992.

"Billy was a little boy who loved horses more than anything in the world." With a first line like that, this children's book was sure to become a classic.

Billy appears to be quite young when his father announces to him one birthday morning that his present is out on the lawn. He finds a beautiful bay pony with four white feet waiting for him there, and the white blaze down his face leaves no doubt as to his name.

Kindred spirits from the beginning, the boy and the horse are together from morning to night, with Billy being responsible for virtually for all his care. They often take long rides through the woods, and on one of these rides, they discover a dog caught in an animal trap. Billy frees him, takes him home and names him Rex, and the three become inseparable companions.

Soon Billy realizes that Blaze can jump effortlessly over almost any obstacle, so when he spots a poster for an upcoming horse show, he decides to enter. He becomes nervous as the other more mature riders take their turns ahead of him. No need to worry though, because Billy, Blaze (and Rex) take the fence easily and earn the silver cup which he proudly displays on the dresser in his bedroom.

Several other Billy & Blaze books are also still currently available from Aladdin Paperbacks, an imprint of Simon & Schuster.

Birthdate—April 12, 1981

SATA—Vol 11 pp.9–12

## 2. Happy Birthday, Moon   Story and pictures by Frank Asch c.1982.

Remember that popular line from Erich Segal's Love Story, "Love means never having to say you're sorry?" Somehow that line has always confused me, because selfless love surely means often having to say you're sorry, as we soon learn in this story.

Bear enjoys chatting with his friend, the moon. He even hikes to the mountains to be closer to the moon when they talk, thus creating an echo, with the moon repeating everything Bear says. The ensuing conversation makes Bear think that the two share an impending birthday. Bear hurries home and dumps "all the money out of his piggy bank." to buy his friend a hat. He dutifully climbs a tree and places it on a branch and waits patiently for the moon to climb up and try it on. During the night, the hat falls out of the tree, and Bear thinks that the moon has given him a hat also. When the wind carries the precious gift away, both protagonists apologize profusely and echo this perfect response, "That's okay, I still love you."

It is obvious from reading this book as well as Asch's many other well-written "Bear" books that the author enjoys an excellent rapport with little ones. Biographical information bears (sorry) this out, as we learn that both he and his wife have been Montessouri teachers.

Here are just a few of his other titles that are still in print—Starjumper (2006), Mooncake (1986) and Moonbear's Shadow (2000).

Birthdate—August 6, 1946

SATA—Vol. 66 pp. 1–10

Fourth Book of Jr. Authors and
  Illustrators—pp. 17–18

## 3. Madeline   Story and pictures by Ludwig Bemelmans c.1939.

The late Ludwig Bemelmans told us in SATA Vol. 15 that he didn't really write Madeline, but rather that "she insisted on being born" during the 41st year of his life.

He was right in that concise summation, of course. A little girl with Madeline's strength of character had to be born in order to delight future generations of children.

She had her beginnings in the stories the author's mother told him about her own childhood in a convent school in Bavaria, but she wasn't really "born" until Bemelmans spent some time in a hospital, subsequently meeting a little girl who had had her appendix out. Interestingly, his hospital room ceiling also had a crack that had "the habit of sometimes looking like a rabbit."

A subtle rhyming text along with the authentic views of Paris by the artist, who once was a waiter in some of New York's finest hotels, have helped this heart-warming story survive for so long.

Other Madeline titles include-Madeline and the Gypsies, Madeline's Rescue, Madeline in London, Madeline's Christmas as well as Madeline and the Bad Hat, a favorite of our eldest daughter.

Birthdate—April 27, 1898–
  d. 1962

SATA—Vol. 15 pp. 15–26

More Jr. Authors—pp. 14–15

## 4. Pelle's New Suit by Elsa Beskow c.1929

In Something About The Author Vol. 17, children's writer Alice Dalgliesh, says "I wonder why we have no American books that are like Pelle's New Suit, a charming book so full of pleasant gardens and flowery meadows that one scarcely suspects it being the story of wool."

Pelle, who appears to be about five, is caring for his lamb as this story opens in a bucolic setting. As the lamb grows, the Swedish boy's suit becomes way too small. The industrious lad takes matters in his own hands and shears his sheep. Both grandmothers help as one cards the wool for him and the other spins it into yarn. Bartering rather than spending, Pelle pulls weeds and tends the cows in exchange for their contributions. He then does an errand for the painter, this acquiring the funds for the dye for his cerulean suit. The book takes us through the other steps in the suit-making process with Pelle even remembering to thank the sheep on the last page.

According to the Jr. Bk. of Authors, Elsa Beskow decided at the age of seven that she would "make picture books" when she grew up. Married at 18, this native of Sweden became the mother of six sons who were models for her stories and eventually her critics as they grew older. Something About the Author tells us that before her death at the age of seventy-nine, she also wrote and illustrated eight collections of fairy tales and thirty-three books. Amazingly, more than 50 years after her death, Beskow still has 15 books in print, including this lovely classic.

Birthdate—February 11, 1874
  d. 1953

SATA—Vol. 20 pp. 13–15

Junior Book of Authors—pp. 30
  & 31.

## 5. Little Gorilla Story and Pictures by Ruth Bornstein c.1976

Needless to say, four year old consultants are very important to me when choosing the books to review for you in this guidebook, so its accurate to say that more than 39 years of research have gone into this book. As I noted in the review for "The Diggingest Dog", our then four-year-old son "made" me read that book to him nearly every afternoon. Recently his four-year-old daughter Mary spent some time at our house, discovered Little Gorilla, and "made" me read it to her several times in one day.

As you can see by the original copyright, Little Gorilla has been around more than 30 years himself, delighting children all the while. Author/illustrator Ruth Bornstein, who was born in Milwaukee, was already married and had four children of her own before he came into being. This was only her second children's book, although she was trained as an artist and had drawn and painted nearly all her life.

"Little Gorilla" took two years to complete, and Bornstein tells us in her SATA biography that "she has always been fascinated with gorillas and wanted to communicate her love for little children (and gorillas) growing big."

Check your encyclopedia and you will find that gorillas, while huge, are quite gentle and peaceable creatures. This message comes across loud and clear as all Little Gorilla's relatives and all the jungle creatures come to admire him when he is "only one day old." Pink Butterfly, Green Parrot and Red Monkey and even Big Boa Constrictor all think Little Gorilla is nice. Giraffe, Young Elephant and Old Elephant, Lion and Old Hippo play with him and love him even after he begins to GROW and GROW. On his birthday he is, of course, quite huge as the jungle creatures all gather for his first birthday party.

Now available as a board book, this selection definitely belongs in your home or school library.

Birthdate—April 28, 1927

SATA—Vol. 88. pp. 44–46

## 6. Clifford, the Small Red Puppy  Story and pictures by Norman Bridwell c.1972.

Clifford's "dad", Norman Bridwell, visited Terre Haute in September of 1983. Clad in red, the genial grandfatherly type entertained an estimated audience of nearly 3000 people. This native Hoosier was born in Kokomo and now lives on Martha's Vineyard.

He told us that Clifford, like a lot of good things, was born out of necessity. At the age of 34, Bridwell found himself to be the starving artist personified with no way to support his wife and daughter, one-year-old Emily Elizabeth. A friend suggested that he write a children's book, based on one of the animal drawings in his file. Clifford was plucked from the group and has been on the move ever since.

In my work with little ones, I have always found that they enjoyed this prequel of Clifford's puppyhood days better than the original book, published six years earlier. Like them, Clifford manages to get himself in quite a few scrapes when he is little, yet he somehow remains maddeningly loveable.

Unfortunately, once his owner, Emily Elizabeth, learns that love and attention will make him grow, he can't seem to stop growing. The problems encountered because of this situation and how it is finally resolved, makes for a very satisfying read-aloud for preschoolers.

Birthdate—February 15, 1928

SATA—Vol. 68 pp.38–39

## 7. Georgie   Story and pictures by Robert Bright c.1944

Yes, yes, I know most stores put their Halloween costumes out earlier and earlier each year, thus annoying their buying public, the very folks they are trying to please. I can't speak for your childhood, but at our house, the five of us managed to pull together an outfit of old clothes or a "ghost sheet" the night before our Halloween party at school, and everything worked out just fine.

In fact, this little story of Georgie the friendly ghost was born during my childhood, back when holidays were perhaps more fun and not so fraught with buying things.

Like a lot of people, Georgie knew his place in life. He lived in a little village in New England. He came downstairs at the same time every night and "gave the loose board on the stair a little creak, and the parlor door a little squeak." At that point the homeowners knew it was time to go to bed and "Herman, the cat, knew it was time to prowl, while Miss Oliver the owl knew it was time to get up."

Havoc is created when Mr. Whitaker bestirs himself to fix that creaky stair, upsetting the entire apple cart, so to speak. After that brief repair job, no one knows when to do anything anymore.

Containing just enough "scariness" for little ones, this still available book is a much better choice than many of the newer Halloween selections.

> Birthdate—August 5, 1902—d. 1988
>
> SATA—Vol. 63, pp.11–13
>
> More Jr. Authors—pp. 28–29

## 8. The Runaway Bunny by Margaret Wise Brown c.1942.

When I was little and got slightly perturbed with my mother, I would always tell her I was going to run away and stay with Aunt Nora. She and Uncle Ed had no children, so I was pretty sure they would take me in. My wise mother made little fuss about these pre-school tirades and so, of course, they soon passed.

The July 26, 1991 issue of Publisher's Weekly tells us that Brown wrote this still popular book during a summer vacation on the island of Vinalhaven off the coast of Maine. Begun the previous summer, it is based upon an old love ballad known to Chaucer in which the lover continues to pursue the beloved, no matter what magical transformations occur.

Mothers are like that, and no matter what my childish outbursts consisted of, I knew that mine still loved me.

In this story, the little bunny threatens to become a fish, a rock on a high mountain, a crocus, a bird, a sailboat, a circus performer, and finally a little boy. Mother Bunny remains calm through all of this, telling him she will pursue him, no matter what.

Some other books by Brown that I especially enjoy are Mister Dog c. 1952, Pussy Willow c. 1951, Little Fur Family c. 1946 and The Big Red Barn c. 1956. The Runaway Bunny, Little Fur Family and The Big Red Barn are also available in newer board book versions.

Birthdate—1910—d. 1952

YABC—Vol. 2

Jr. Book of Authors—p.55

## 9. Grandfather and I by Helen E. Buckley. c.1959

Now that my husband and I have three grandchildren, we have learned a lot. For example, we have learned that you can give them back to their parents after experiencing the pleasure of their company for a while. This is quite preferable to the 24 hour a day job that parenting entails.

Helen Elizabeth Buckley had had absolutely no grandparenting experience when she published this thought-provoking book more than 40 years ago. She taught nursery school and kindergarten, however, and had an excellent grasp of the world as seen through the eyes of a small boy. The well-dressed nameless young man in the story relishes his walk with Grandfather, since he is the only relative in his life that never hurries. They always "walk along and walk along and stop…and look…just as long as we like." Mothers and fathers hurry and brothers and sisters " are always leaving you far behind."

One of the late Paul Galdone's first efforts at illustration, this true classic has recently been issued in hard back at $14.95 and deserves an honored place in your child's library.

A paperback version is also available for this book as well as Grandmother and I published in 1961.

Proving once again that some of the best children's writers only improve with age, Buckley published "Moonlight Kite" when she was 79. It is still available as well and is a little more suitable for your six, seven or eight year old.

Birthdate—June 6, 1918

SATA—Vol. 2 pp. 38 & 39

## 10. The Little House  Story and pictures by Virginia Lee Burton c.1942.

Does the dream of a cottage in the country rest in the heart of nearly every person as it does in me? The penciled house plans never vary much and the location of some land not far from the farm of my birth in Wisconsin remains constant, too. It will be "strong and well built" just like The Little House, and perhaps; just perhaps, our great grandchildren might live there some day.

In this classic book, The Little House sits on a hill and watches the sun rise and set, the moon in all its phases, and the months, seasons, and years pass, all the while wondering what it would be like to live in the city. She finds out all too soon as automobiles, trucks and subdivisions begin to encroach upon her once peaceful environment. She is soon surrounded by high rises, traffic and street noise and begins to miss her country home. She becomes sad, lonely and neglected, until the great-great-grand-daughter of the original owner returns her to her idyllic countryside. She is repaired and lived in once more and "never again would she be curious about the city."

Mike Mulligan and His Steam Shovel and Katy and the Big Snow are two of the author's other well-known books that are still in print.

The daughter of the first dean of MIT, Virginia Lee Burton substantiates my theory that the writers of quality books for children are bright people.

Birthdate—August 30, 1909—d. 1968

SATA—Vol. 2 pp. 42–44

Jr. Book of Authors—p. 62

## 11. The Grouchy Ladybug   Story and pictures by Eric Carle c.1977

Unlike 98% of all Americans, two of my former preschool students did not have a TV set in their home. Their mother had a master's degree in nursing and wanted to help the boys and their older siblings learn to appreciate good books.

Her plan worked. Few children in my five years of teaching preschool were better listeners than those two tow-heads. In fact, the three year old had this book nearly memorized after hearing it only once. He hurried through his snack, rushed back to the rug, retrieved it from the pile and "read" it back to us.

No wonder! Carle's masterpiece contains all the important elements of a great picture book, and was a mainstay of our Bugs (insects, if you prefer) unit every September at school. It teaches children about ladybugs and aphids and telling time and mixes it all in with a lesson on how to get along in the world, even if you are very small and more than a little grouchy.

You really can't go wrong when choosing any of Carle's books, but try this one on your preschoolers and see if they don't like it a bit better than the author's wildly popular The Very Hungry Caterpillar, published when he was 50 years old.

Birthdate—June 25, 1929.

SATA—Vol. 65, pp. 30–36

4th Book of Jr. Authors & Illustrators—pp. 68–69

## 12. Jesse Bear, What Will You Wear? By Nancy White Carlstrom c.1986

Of all the children's authors that I have reviewed over the past five years, Nancy White Carlstrom ranks very high on my list of authors that I would like to meet. Why, you may ask? She holds the record for most rejections before getting a book published...82!

However, we are so glad that her persistence paid off. She received word on her son's second birthday that Jesse Bear would be published by Macmillan.

She also tells us in SATA—Vol. 53, that she wants the words of her books "to flow off the page and be easy for young children to repeat." She certainly succeeded in this first book in a series of Jesse Bear adventures.

Like many preschoolers, Jesse Bear can't decide what to wear upon arising, so he becomes whimsically philosophical as he repeats rhymes such as-

> "I'll wear a rose
>
> Between my toes
>
> A rose in my toes in the morning."

Bruce Degan's illustrations of the nearly idyllic bear family will not only make you want to purchase the book, but you may even want to build a house exactly like their cozy cottage.

Several other books about the vivacious Jesse Bear have now been published and your child will enjoy them too. Some of the titles are—Better Not Get Wet, Jesse Bear, Happy Birthday, Jesse Bear, and It's About Time, Jesse Bear.

Birthdate—August 4, 1948

SATA—Vol. 53, pp. 19–21

Jr. Book of Authors—Vol. 6. pp. 48—49

## 13. Miss Rumphius Story and pictures by Barbara Cooney c.1982

Like Miss Rumphius herself, Barbara Cooney just kept getting better and better as she aged, giving us all hope for the future. She was illustrator for The Man Who Didn't Wash His Dishes in 1950, a clever little story by Phyllis Krasilovsky, which in also included in this book. However, there is no comparison between those illustrations and the ones in this selection or Hattie and the Wild Waves, an excellent choice for your first or second grader.

So what is your ultimate goal in life? Even as a child, Miss Alice Rumphius knew that she would one day go to faraway places and live by the sea when she grew old. Her wise grandfather reminded her that she must also "do something to make the world more beautiful."

Accomplishing her first two goals was easy enough, as she became a librarian and traveled to the mountains, desert and jungle on her vacations. Later in life, she built her "place by the sea" and "started a little garden among the rocks." She "was almost perfectly happy."

Like many of us, Miss Rumphius eventually learned that planting flowers gave her and others a great deal of pleasure. Lupines became her flower of choice and she ultimately planted "five bushels" of the very best seed.

I hope they are still blooming when I finally get to vacation in Maine.

Birthdate—August 6, 1917

SATA—Vol. 59. pp. 46–54

More Jr. Authors—pp. 53–54.

Books Are By People—
    pp.41–43.

## 14. Freight Train  Story and pictures by Donald Crews c.1978

More than 60 trains passed through our former city of Terre Haute daily, irritating adults who were always rushing to get somewhere. However, trains were nearly always a fascinating joy to young children, especially the boys.

So please, if you have a boy between the ages of two and five, buy him this book. Many young girls love anything that moves too, so if you have one of those unique daughters, buy it for her as well.

This Caldecott Honor book is just right for little ones containing 55 large print, well-chosen words. The bold bright colors on the uncluttered pages are perfect, and somehow the talented Crews has made his young readers feel as if a freight train is actually moving through the 22 pages. He shows us the empty track first, then the red caboose, orange tank car, yellow hopper car, green cattle car, blue gondola car, purple box car, a black tender and a black steam engine. If you have to grab your dictionary and look up "hopper," "gondola" and "tender", that is good, too. The best books for even the youngest children are never watered down, but rather stretch the child's vocabulary with large, correct, fascinating words. Small children love big words.

You can read this book aloud in a minute or two, so it would make a great baby gift, as it will never wear out or need batteries.

Crews, the father of two children, was born in Newark, New Jersey, but developed his love for trains while he and his siblings were spending summers at his grandmother's farm in Cottondale, Florida. This is also the basis for Bigmama's (1991), a great read-aloud story for slightly older children.

Crews received his second Caldecott Honor award for

Truck (1981) and has lots of other great books still in print also.

Birthdate—August 30, 1938

SATA—Vol. 76 pp. 41–45

## 15. Charlie Needs A Cloak   Story and Pictures by Tomie de Paola c.1973

If you love old children's books as I do, you will scour book sales, garage sales and antique stores until you find "Pelle's New Suite" by Elsa Beskow (c. 1929). I found my hardback copy for 50 cents at our library book sale a few years ago and have included it in this anthology.

It will be a great companion to this more modern classic by the incomparable Tomie de Paola. In this book, Charlie is a poor little shepherd boy with a crook and lots of fat sheep to attend to, but you can tell by the picture of the very first page that he definitely needs a new cloak. So in the spring, he begins by shearing his sheep. Then he washes the wool and cards it to straighten it out. He spins the wool into yarn, and since he wants a red cloak; he must pick some pokeweed berries in the late summer, so he can boil them to make the red dye. He puts the strands of red yarn on his loom and begins to spend his fall evenings weaving the yarn into cloth. He cuts the pieces of cloth, pins them carefully and finally sews it all together by hand in the evenings in front of the fireplace. When the snow begins to fall as it does every winter, Charlie dons his fine new cloak looking very smug, as one of the sheep gnaws holes in the hem, unbeknownst to Charlie.

Your children will love the fact that this same sheep and a very obliging mouse have helped him out on every page during the cloak-making process.

Birthdate—September 15, 1934

SATA—Vol. 108 pp. 59–72.

## 16. Pancakes For Breakfast by Tomie de Paola
## c.1978

Now what could be better than pancakes on a cold winter morning? Not much, the nameless round lady decides as she wakes up on just such a frosty morning. The cat and dog look on as she ties on her apron, finds her recipe and sets about gathering all her ingredients. Of course, they must be fresh, so her cat and dog watch as she gathers eggs from the hens and sits on her three-legged stool to milk her cow. Her formerly happy face begins to show some dismay as she spends quite a long time churning the milk into butter. Once she has that completed, she discovers that there is absolutely no maple syrup, and what are fresh pancakes without fresh maple syrup? She dons her perky little hat and shawl and sets off to buy maple syrup from a nearby farmer, leaving the cat and dog home alone. Big mistake~ The animals are hungry too, and devour the fresh ingredients while she is gone. The very funny and talented de Paola adds a humorous twist at the end of the book, as the industrious little lady gets a whiff of her neighbor's pancakes. Off she goes uninvited. Formality doesn't bother her a bit. She soon devours a huge pile of their pancakes and goes happily home completely stuffed.

Your three, four, or five year old will be quite willing to tell his or her own version of this nearly wordless book.

The jovial, grandfatherly de Paola, whom I once had the privilege of meeting at Kid's Ink here in Indianapolis, currently has many books still in print, including Strega Nona-a Caldecott Honor Book in 1975.

Birthdate—September 15, 1934

SATA—Vol. 108 pp. 59–72

## 17. Jamberry   Story and Pictures by Bruce Degan c.1983.

While I seldom consider it necessary to enhance a well-written book with visual aids, we almost always served at least three kinds of berries for snack when we enjoyed this book at our preschool.

Even though Degan was born in Brooklyn, he tells us in his author's note on the last page of this delicious gem that he picked berries as a child in the pastures with his grandparents on their farm.

The happy memories practically jump off the page as the author feeds us verses like-

"Hatberry

Shoeberry

In my canoeberry"

As the boy and the bear paddle wildly down the river.

The book doesn't really have a complicated plot, nor does it need one, as a small rather perplexed boy and a large brown bear spend a warm late summer day together among various berry patches. Looking at the pictures more carefully, you realize that there are marshmallows growing along the river and cookies posing as lily pads, while bread slices grow in the nearby trees. The bear and the boy frolic among blueberry, strawberry and blackberry patches while riding down a river in a canoe, dancing around a maypole with a myriad of animals and riding a trainful of berries, which sports a goose as the engineer. If all this sounds a bit silly, it is, and that is exactly why your little one will love it.

Thankfully, Jamberry is now available as a board book, as are many of the other classics reviewed in this anthology.

Degan is also the illustrator for the Magic School Bus

series for slightly older children and of course the incomparable Jesse Bear stories as well,

One of his more recent books, Sailaway Home (1996), which took him about a year to write, is also perfect for preschoolers.

Birthdate—June 14, 1945.

SATA—Vol. 57 pp.47–52

6th Book of Jr. Authors and
   Ill.—pp 75 and 76

## 18. Flip   Story and Pictures by Wesley Dennis c.1941

"Flip was born." Don't you love that classic line of this 56 year-old book? How else would you begin a story about a feisty little colt?

Other than the Billy and Blaze series by C.W. Anderson, I can't think of any books, old or new, that will satisfy your young horse lover more than this one. In fact, our musty orange paperback copy still contains our oldest daughter's name in her first grade hand, and some of the pages are precariously loose from overuse.

Young children are often frustrated by their size and inability to do things, and I believe that is the main reason why this book has endured. No matter how often or how hard he tries, Flip simply cannot jump over the brook that flows through his peaceful domain. Frustrated and exhausted from trying, he falls asleep in the sunshine beside the brook one afternoon. He dreams he has silver wings and can jump anywhere, even over the barn. Buoyed by this inspiration, can you guess what he accomplishes upon arising?

Dennis once worked as a portrait painter at Filene's in Boston, among many other occupations before gaining success at 38 with Flip, his first children's book.

Unfortunately, as of this writing, Flip is out of print. Hopefully, some astute publisher will reissue it soon, preferably as a board book.

Birthdate—May 16, 1903 d. 1966

SATA—Vol. 18 pp.70–74

More Jr. Authors—pp. 64–65

## 19. May I Bring A Friend? by Beatrice Schenk De Regniers. c.1964.

French born illustrator Beni Montresor won the Caldecott Medal for his illustrations for this childhood fantasy, and luckily the quality of a story matches the excellence of the pictures in this medal winner.

It is quite true in this case, as a small boy on the very first page, nattily attired in his Little Lord Faulteleroy outfit, receives an invitation to join the King and Queen for tea. Being royalty, they politely agreed when he asked if he could bring a friend; they just didn't expect it to be a giraffe. The giraffe was quite well-behaved, and so the hosts asked the boy if he could come and eat stew with them on Sunday evening. Regrettably, they agree to let him bring a friend, who turns out to be a hot pink rhinoceros this time. Naturally, he eats everything. The friends are plural on Tuesday and produce a lot of monkey business, hanging from the chandelier, etc. Undaunted, the King and Queen ask the boy to come again on Wednesday, and he arrives in regal splendor atop a pink elephant. After completing the week with a few more outrageous houseguests, a much more comfortable home is found for the animals on Saturday, as we visit the zoo and find them there at the end of the book.

DeRegniers and I have several things in common, although I've never met her. She was born in Lafayette, Indiana, just about an hour's drive from our former home in Terre Haute. She loves the out-of-doors, often taking her paper and pencil outside, if she feels she really needs to concentrate. And finally, she saves her Mondays for writing, even though her other days are often spent in other pursuits.

The paperback book that I have was only $4.95; so do add this delightful fantasy to your home library.

Birthdate—August 16, 1914

SATA—Vol. 68 pp. 62–65.

## 20. Are You My Mother?   Story and pictures by P.D. Eastman c.1960

A giant in the children's book publishing era of the 1960's when our children were young, the late Philip Dey Eastman still has several books in print today.

So a dilemma has occurred. Shall I tell you about this book or his still available 1968 gem The Best Nest? Our family copies of both hardbacks are limp from overuse, and they were quite popular in my preschool class as well.

Perhaps you can consult your own 4 year old, who may prefer this one because of the SNORT. Then hustle down to the library and retrieve this book.

As this 64 page I Can Read It All By Myself Beginner Book opens, Mother Bird is sitting on a lone egg which has begun to crack. Panicking, she realizes there is nothing in the house (pardon me, nest) for him to eat, so she ventures off to find a worm or two. She is gone a long time and naturally, he chooses this time to be born. Now it's his turn to panic, as he realizes there is no mother about. Falling out of the nest, the undaunted, albeit flightless, baby proceeds on foot for exactly twenty pages questioning in turn a kitten, hen, dog, cow, an old car, a boat and finally, a plane flying overhead, wondering whether or not they are his mother. All indignantly or silently decline.

He then encounters a big red and yellow thing. Running brazenly up to it, he asks if it is his mother, whereupon it says "SNORT." The "SNORT" (really a giant steam shovel) picks him up and transports him along until he is finally deposited back to—you guessed it-his own nest, where he is warmly welcomed by his formerly distraught mother.

Birthdate—November 25, 1909
d. 1986

SATA—Vol. 33 pp. 56–57

## 21. Play With Me   Story and Pictures by Marie Hall Ets. c.1955

If you were to tell me that your preschooler was one of the loveable but lively types and you wanted me to suggest the perfect picture book to help settle him or her down just a bit, I would recommend this one.

Based on Mrs. Ets' childhood years in Wisconsin's north woods, it is the story of a little girl looking for a friend (and aren't we all?). Like a lot of us, however, she does just a bit too much "pursuing" as she chases after forest creatures, hoping they will play with her.

Dejected, she sits down on a rock beside a pond and quietly watches a bug in the water. She continues to sit there without making a sound, and one by one the birds and animals come back to play with her, rewarding her for her solitude and listening skills.

Named a Caldecott Honor Book in 1956, it is still available in paperback as a picture Puffin for a mere $5.99.

In his landmark 1969 book about the lives of children's authors, Books Are By People, Lee Bennett Hopkins described the 74 year-old Ets as having a robust personality. She explained when she talked to him that she hoped her 1960 Caldecott Medal winner, Nine Days to Christmas, would give a more accurate view of the way Mexican children actually lived. Other popular books by Ets that are still in print in include: Gilberto and the Wind (c. 1963) and In the Forest (c.1944), a Caldecott Honor Book.

Birthdate—December 16, 1895.

SATA—Vol. 2 pp. 102, 105.

Junior Book of Authors—pp. 115–116

Books Are By People—pp. 61–63.

## 22. Angus and the Cat   Story and Pictures by Marjorie Flack c.1931

Marjorie Flack's trilogy about her little black Scottish Terrier makes choosing just one a very tough call, so please get them all if you have anyone under six residing with you.

The cats in our lives would never forgive me, however, if I didn't choose this one as my personal favorite. Out of the three, it is perhaps the most clever, as the incident of the cat hiding on the roof is based on a true incident in the Flack household.

Angus is still in his puppyhood days as this story begins, and he is curious about "MANY THINGS", especially "CATS". However, traveling on a leash, he can't really learn much about them, until one truly astonishes him by appearing on his own turf. The two antagonize each other for "THREE WHOLE DAYS" until she slips out on the roof and disappears. Hmmmm! Now what will Angus do?

Be sure to look for the other two, Angus Lost (1932) and Angus and the Ducks (1930) which led to another of Flack's well-known books The Story of Ping (1933). One of her other books which was always a big hit in our preschool was Ask Mr. Bear (1932) which is also included in this anthology.

> Birthdate—October 23, 1897 d. 1958
>
> Jr. Book of Authors—pp. 127–128
>
> Yesterday's Authors of Books for Children—Vol. 2 page 123

## 23. Ask Mr. Bear   Story and pictures by Marjorie Flack c.1932

When I was a child, my brothers and sister and I managed to amuse ourselves quite well nearly every summer with a bat, a ball and an assortment of rather flat and beat up baseball gloves. Whenever a gift-giving occasion arose, such as a birthday or Mother's Day, a homemade card and some wildflowers were the order of the day. In contrast, I recently visited the home of a family who had only one child under the age of two, and the future dining room was entirely filled with his toys. Sometimes the norm today, this was not true in 1932, when the small golden-haired boy in this book has no money at all and is trying to come up with a birthday gift for his mother. Danny decides to enlist the help of the animals and begins by asking the hen who offers an egg. Since Mother already has an egg, they skip along together until they meet the goose, who says she can give him some feathers for a fine pillow. Since she has a pillow and also some cheese proposed by the goat and a wool blanket which the sheep is willing to give, Danny and all the animals continue on together until they meet the pleasant cow in the meadow. Naturally she offers milk and cheese that Mother also has. She suggests that he ask Mr. Bear in the woods. Not surprisingly, none of the animals are willing to press on with this part of the journey, but Mr. Bear offers Danny the best suggestion of all, which you'll simply have to read about yourself.

Several versions of this book are still available including a $5.99 paperback.

Although Flack died more than forty years ago, all three of the Angus books, as well as her 1946 Caldecott Honor Book. The Boats On the River, illustrated by her son-in-law and The Story About Ping (1933) are still in print. Ping is another not-to-be-missed story, but it is a bit longer and a little more suitable for first and second graders.

Birthdate—October 23, 1897 d. 1958

SATA—Vol. 100 pp. 91–94

## 24. Poems to Read to the Very Young Selected by Josette Frank c.1961

My friend, children's writer Bette Killion, who has the gift of writing poetry with great ease, would never let me write an anthology of children's books such as this one without including as least one poetry collection. Neither would the now deceased poetry legend Aileen Fisher, whom I had the privilege of interviewing in her Boulder home in April 1996.

Born in 1906, Fisher was one of the liveliest, most intelligent conversationalists I have ever met, and I was quite reluctant to leave after our 45 minute chat.

The Random House Pictureback contains 43 poems by lots of "giants" in the field such as Rose Fyleman, Vachel Lindsay, A.A. Milne, Rachel Field, Marchette Chute, Laura E. Richards, Walter de la Mare, Christina G. Rosette, Gilette Burgess, and of course, Miss Fisher.

Additionally, even though the book is more than forty years old, children continue to tell me that it's their favorite. In fact, a second-grader at Pine Tree Elementary in Avon, Indiana, Jacqueline Trout, once told me this was her favorite book "loving it since I was a baby."

Finally, it contains my favorite four-line stanza by our old friend, Anonymous:

> "I'm glad the sky is painted blue,
>
> And the earth is painted green,
>
> With such a lot of nice fresh air
>
> All sandwiched in between."

Frank was such an expert in the field of children's literature that her obituary ran in the New York Times on September 14, 1989. SATA tells us that she was married, had two children and worked variously as a consultant, administrator, editor, and lecturer in addition to her writing.

> Birthdate—March 27, 1893, d. 1989.
>
> SATA—Vol. 10, p. 47— Obituary Vol.63, p.34.

## 25. Corduroy   Story and pictures by Don Freeman c.1968

When I taught first grade in Terre Haute, Corduroy lived in our room. Arrayed in his authentic green corduroys he resided in a basket and got to go home each evening with a child who had had an especially good day.

We hadn't had him long when he lost one of his white buttons, causing his normally cheerful demeanor to appear to sadden a bit. When it was Pam Bender's turn to take him home, he returned the next day with a spanking new white button, sewn on by Pam's grandmother. Hopefully, she didn't have to search as hard for the white button as the original Corduroy in the story did.

When Lisa and her mother initially spot him in the store he is missing a button, so Mother tries to dissuade her daughter from buying a bear that "doesn't look new." During the evening while the small bear searches all over the department store for his missing fastener, Lisa counts what she has saved in her piggy bank. She appears bright and early the next morning at the department store to retrieve the bear, and takes him home to sew a button on so he will be "more comfortable."

A one time professional trumpet player, Freeman wrote lots of books that your children will enjoy, including Dandelion, A Rainbow of My Own and Mop Top. In fact, he has twelve books still listed in the 2005 version of Children's Books in Print. A Pocket for Corduroy was in production when he died in 1978.

> Birthdate—August 11, 1908—d. 1978
>
> SATA—Vol. 17 pp. 60–69
>
> More Jr. Authors—pp. 90–91
>
> Books are By People—pp. 78–81

## 26. Millions of Cats   Story and pictures by Wanda Gag. c.1928.

This is one of those rare picture books which was named as a Newbery Honor Book, and the quality of the story line tells us why. Obviously the very old man and the very old lady care deeply about one another as the story opens in their cozy hut. They are lonely, nevertheless, and the wife expresses her desire for a cat. Her husband happily sets off over the hills to find her one. As luck would have it, instead he finds "hundreds of cats, thousands of cats, millions and billions and trillions of cats." Unable to decide among them, he takes them all home to his astonished wife. A melee ensues, as they decide to let the cats themselves choose which of them is the prettiest. Finally, only one scraggly little cat is left. The love and attention that the couple heaps upon him soon makes him grow "nice and plump" and indeed he becomes "the most beautiful cat in the whole world", at least according to the very old man, a feline expert in anyone's book.

Children love the repetitiveness of "hundreds of cats, thousands, millions and billions and trillions of cats, "but I also think that they identify with the modest "very homely little cat" who blossoms under the love and care of the childless couple.

Amazingly this book was initially rejected by several New York publishers, as were The Funny Thing and Snippy and Snappy, also penned by the author.

Miss Gag, a friend of Georgia O'Keefe, supported her younger siblings with her work, and all six of them lived with her at one time or another.

Birthdate—March 11, 1893 d. 1946

Junior Book of Authors—pp. 134–136

## 27. The Teeny, Tiny Woman   Illustrated and Retold by Paul Galdone. c.1984

Born in Budapest Hungary, Paul Galdone emigrated to the United States with his family, settling in New Jersey while still in high school. A bit of a laughing stock as he attempted to read Shakespeare in English, the artistically talented Galdone became a hero to his schoolmates when he offered to draw their grasshoppers for them in biology class. SATA Vol. 17 also tells us that like many authors and illustrators, he toiled at a myriad of jobs before finding his niche. While still a young man, he moved with his family to New York City, where he attended art class at night and worked during the day.

I seldom made suggestions as to how my husband should proceed with his work in economic development, and likewise he rarely insisted that I review certain books for my newspaper column. This special English folktale was an exception however, and he recited the entire story for me, remembering it from his childhood. When we found this large print copy at our world famous Children's Museum here in Indianapolis, he insisted I buy it.

The thatched roofed English cottages and profuse flower gardens set the scene where "There was a teeny-tiny woman who lived in a teeny-tiny house in a teeny-tiny village." In fact defying one of the cardinal rules of writing to never repeat the same word or phrase too much, "teeny-tiny" is repeated 63 times to the sheer delight of young children. Galdone's whimsical drawings add much to the tale as the diminutive protagonist finds a bone in the churchyard cemetery and proceeds to take it home in the hope of making soup with it. Her slumber is disturbed several times by a frightening voice insisting in louder and louder tomes "Give me my bone!" Finally, giving your young listening audience a chance to shout in school without recrimination, she bellows "TAKE IT!"

Birthdate—June 2, 1914 d. 1986

SATA—Vol. 17 pp. 69–75.

## 28. The Little Red Hen   Adapted and Illustrated by Paul Galdone c.1973.

Louisa May Alcott once said, "Work is my salvation and I will celebrate it." I've often felt that way myself, since there is a great deal of joy in being able to physically and mentally accomplish or complete a task.

Thankfully, the Little Red Hen felt the same way, since her housemates, the cat, the dog and the mouse preferred sleeping all day, leaving her to do literally all the work. She "cooked the meals, washed the dishes and made the beds." Then "she swept the floor and washed the windows and mended the clothes." After that, she did virtually all the yard work as well.

She found some grains of wheat one day while hoeing the garden and proceeded to plant it herself, since no one would help. Then as you know, but your three or four year old probably doesn't, she also has to cut the wheat, take it to the mill to be ground into flour, and make the cake herself. Her unambitious roommates helped with none of these tasks, but guess who turned up to help her eat it? Wisely, she tells them she plans to eat it all herself, but Galdone adds a twist at the end of the book that I especially like. On the very last page, he shows the cat, the dog and the mouse busily tidying up the house with rather sheepish looks on their faces.

Galdone found a great deal of satisfaction in adapting and illustrating old tales for little ones, and many are still listed in the 2005 version of Children's Books in Print.

In the Third Book of Jr. Authors, Galdone mentioned that he had worked for 25 different publishers. Living in Greenwich Village as a young man, he eventually married and had two children. He did his writing and illustrating on his farm in Vermont before his death in 1986 at the age of 72.

Birthdate—June 2, 1914 d. 1986

SATA—Vol. 17 pp. 69–75

## 29. Be Nice to Spiders   Story and pictures by Margaret Bloy Graham c.1967

Poor Billy! His family is moving to a new apartment that doesn't allow pets, and he can't take his eight-legged arachnid companion, Helen.

He leaves the foundling at the doorstep of the zoo, where she happily begins to devour all the flies that have been annoying the animals. This arrangement pleases all concerned until the mayor announces an impending visit. Tidying up the place, the keepers eradicate all visible spider webs, and Helen hides in the camel house, narrowly escaping with her life. After the visit, only the camels are content, as the flies begin to once more annoy the other four-legged residents. Puzzled, the zookeepers finally realize that they should "be nice to spiders." Helen obligingly produces an egg sac with lots of babies, and peace is restored to the zoo once more.

A native of Toronto, Canada, Graham tells us in More Junior Authors that as a child, she loved drawing more than reading and was encouraged in that endeavor by one of her high school teachers. Married to children's author Gene Zion for many years, she collaborated with him on a number of his books including Harry, the Dirty Dog, also in this anthology.

Birthdate—November 2, 1920

SATA—Vol. 11 pp. 119–120.

More Junior Authors—pp. 102–103

## 30. Little Toot   Story and Pictures by Hardie Gramatky c.1939

It seems to me that nearly all writers and would-be writers have several projects rolling around in their heads all at the same time. I am no exception to this premise, and one of my recurring aspirations is to rewrite this wonderful story, editing it quite a bit to make it a little more suitable for today's children.

There is no way that anyone could improve on the storyline, however. Displaying an excessive amount of hubris, the small tugboat puffs around the New York harbor emitting his tiny toots "feeling very important" and accomplishing little else. His father, however, Big Toot works extremely hard, and Grandfather Toot also loves to tell "of his mighty deeds on the river."

Like some other young folks, though, Little Toot does not relish physical labor. He spends his days playing imaginative games in the calm harbor to the derision of the larger hard-working tugs. When he finally decides to do a little work, his reputation has preceded him, and none of the ships want his help. Self-pity absorbs him as he inadvertently floats out into the "Great Ocean" with a storm approaching. Becoming aware of his surroundings, he realizes that one of the great ocean liners is caught between two rocks. What to do? Thinking fast, he begins to puff an SOS out of his minute smokestack and a "great fleet" of ships appears. However, they are unable to get to the trapped ship, and Little Toot must complete the rescue himself. He becomes a hero as "Grandfather Toot blasts the news all over the river."

Birthdate—April 12, 1970 d, 1979

SATA—Vol. 30. pp. 116–123

Junior Book of Authors—pp. 142 & 143

Books Are By People—pp. 91–93.

## 31. Nobody Listens to Andrew by Elizabeth Guilfoile. c.1957.

In his landmark 1936 book, How to Win Friends and Influence People, Dale Carnegie tells us that few of us really listen to each other. Most of us are much more concerned with ourselves and what we are going to say next, rather than actively listening to the person who has the floor at the moment. Lamentably, where young people are concerned, this fact seems to be twice as common.

In this book, the youngest child in the family is virtually ignored when he attempts to tell his family that there is something black on his bed on the sun porch. One by one, his four family members ignore him, concentrating on their own concerns of the moment.

Finally, Andrew stamps his foot and shouts, "There is a bear upstairs in my bed." He gets his longed-for attention as the police, the fireman, the dogcatcher and the man from the zoo all arrive simultaneously.

Incidentally, this tale like many excellent stories, is based on real events that took place one summer in Minnesota, so please keep that in mind the next time you are tempted to ignore your preschooler.

Winner of the Follett Beginning to Read Award, this book "has a total vocabulary of only 102 words" and was tested on first grade classes, "where children read it with delight and were very unwilling to part with it," according to information printed on the back of this book.

After an exhaustive search, I have found no biographical information about this author, other than the fact that she was once a member of the National Council of Teachers of English. If any of you readers have further information about her, I would love to hear from you.

## 32. Jessica   Story and pictures by Kevin Henkes c.1989.

K evin Henkes is the only author featured in this anthology who is wearing a letter jacket in his "Something About The Author" biography. Hopefully, this will remind you that he was only 19 when he went to New York with his portfolio and an insatiable desire to write and illustrate children's books. Approaching it like a man 30 years older, the Racine, Wisconsin native had thoroughly researched his subject. Thus, he landed a contract with Greenwillow (his first choice) just a few days after his arrival. He remains with that publishing company, now a part of Harper Collins, and continues to produce approximately one book a year of extremely high quality.

Although I've truly enjoyed all his books, I'm quite partial to the invisible protagonist, Jessica. Her real life friend, almost Kindergartner, Ruthie, is a very bright child. To her, Jessica is quite real indeed, accompanying her to the table, the playground and virtually everywhere else. Even though her parents shout, "There is no Jessica!" she continues to fulfill her much needed, albeit temporary, role. Like nearly all high quality picture books, this one ends with a clever twist.

A versatile writer, Henkes has also penned several novels for older children as well as a number of other picture books, including the hilarious A Weekend With Wendell, an excellent choice for your six or seven year old. Be sure to track down "The Biggest Boy" too, if you do have a preschooler in your household.

Birthdate—November 27, 1960

SATA—Vol. 43 pp.119–112

## 33. The Country Bunny and the Little Gold Shoes by DuBose Heyward. c.1939.

Growing up on a farm in Wisconsin, my siblings and I never questioned the fact that chores were a normal part of the day. While it has been quite some time since I milked those Holsteins by hand, the daily work ethic stayed with me.

In this, his only children's book, Heyward, a playwright, teaches all of us some very valuable lessons about the work ethic and the rearing of children.

Parenting expert John Rosemond and others often lament the fact that the lack of such expectations for today's children is the reason for a myriad of evils, such as poor school grades and over-crowded prisons.

The wise country bunny in this story certainly never vacillates in her role as teacher with her children. Prefacing her lessons with the words "Now we are going to have some fun," she teaches all 21 of her children certain household tasks. Once they master these tasks, they are expected to do them daily, freeing her up to pursue her lifelong goal of becoming an Easter Bunny. In addition to her regular duties, she is also given the task of delivering a special egg to an ill boy who lives on top of a mountain. How will her tired feet transport her?

Grandfather Bunny appears at her side with a tiny pair of gold shoes which magically convey her on her mission of mercy. After completing this task, she returns home to find her country cottage neat and tidy, just as she expected it would be.

Although this classic is longer than most of today's picture books, it should not be missed and can certainly be read aloud to a three, four, or five year old in a on-on-one situation.

Birthdate—August 31, 1885 d.
1940.

SATA—Vol. 21 pp. 66–69

## 34. Bedtime For Frances by Russell Hoban c.1960

"U is for underwear, down in the dryer."

If the above quote is in your bank of childhood read-aloud memories, then you probably heard this story many times, just as our own three children did.

Although we can only guess which one of Hoban's seven children was the model for the indomitable young badger-child, it may well have been the first one. Frances is actually an only child in this classic, and she takes full advantage of this situation in her nightly bedtime ritual.

Even if you surmise your preschooler to be a "pro" at such stalling, he or she could certainly take lessons from Frances. In turn, she asks for a glass of milk, a piggyback ride to bed, her teddy bear, her doll, two kisses, then two more kisses and finally permission to have her door open. WHEW!

Still unable to sleep, she sings the afore-mentioned alphabet song with its famous underwear line. There is also a tiger in her room and a giant! She cons her folks out of a piece of cake, brushes her teeth and imagines a creature coming through the crack in her ceiling. (Impressive, huh?) All ends well as Frances finally learns it is her "job" to go to sleep!

Even though Hoban didn't publish this title, his first book for children, until he was 35, his earlier work in New York for such magazines as Time, Life and The Saturday Evening Post, surely contributed to it's success. Thankfully he has persevered, writing numerous children's books including five titles about Frances the irrepressible badger.

Birthdate—February 4, 1925.

SATA—Vol. 78 pp. 81–87.

3rd Book of Junior Authors—
    pp. 129–130.

## 35. Danny and the Dinosaur   Story and pictures by Syd Hoff c.1958.

Hide and Seek is the only children's game that is played in cultures all over the world, a bit of trivia that I learned recently by listening to a morning radio show. They explained that since no props are needed, children of all races and cultures can enjoy it, even the poorest of children.

Perhaps that is one of the reasons for the popularity of this nearly 50-year-old book. After Danny visits some of the exhibits at a nearby museum, he finally arrives at the DINOSAUR! exhibit, his favorite, of course. When he voices the opinion that he would like a dinosaur to play with, the dinosaur surprises him by saying that he would like to play with him too! Off they go to explore the city with Danny riding atop his back. They try to climb a few skyscrapers, help an old lady with her bundles, watch a ball game, swim in the river, eat ice cream and go to the zoo. Finally, Danny goes to look for his friends who are thrilled with his new pet. They teach him a lot of tricks including how to shake hands and roll over. But-you guessed it-they have the most fun playing hide and seek. The children are much more successful at hiding than the dinosaur is, because how do you hide a dinosaur anyway? Nevertheless, the dinosaur decides it's the most fun he's had in a "hundred million years" and then calmly goes back to the museum where he belongs.

Hoff, who died at the age of 91 in May 2004, was born in the Bronx and once aspired to be a fine artist, enrolling in the National Academy of Design in New York at a very young age. However his obituary in the Indianapolis Star tells us that he once said the "a natural comic touch in my work caused my harried instructor to advise me to try something else."

In addition to his work as a cartoonist for the New

Yorker for more than 40 years, Hoff also wrote and illustrated a great many books for young children. "Sammy the Seal" was another staple in our household, so do look for that one too.

Birthdate—September 14, 1912

SATA—Vol. 72 pp.114–118

## 36. The Littlest Leaguer by Syd Hoff c.1976.

I can still remember those summer mornings when we began our farm chores about 4:30 in order to take the four hour drive to Milwaukee to watch Eddie Mathews and Hank Aaron hit those back to back homers for the Braves during the 1950's. Such childhood memories tend to stay with one forever, so even though any and all of Hoff's cartoon-like creations would be excellent for your child, this one is definitely my favorite.

The fact that our youngest daughter was the smallest one on her Miss Softball America team in Terre Haute for four years may also contribute to my love for the hapless Harold. Big Leon, the powerful first baseman was the bane of Harold's existence as he tried out for position after for position to no avail. Hoping to cheer Harold up, the coach even called upon the family one evening to tell about all the short players in the Baseball Hall of Fame, such as Pee Wee Reese. In the top of the ninth, with the bases loaded, in the final game of the season, Harold finally gets his chance as he steps up to bat for the injured Big Leon. Harold "swung with all his might" and any true baseball lover knows what happened next!

Birthdate—September 4, 1912
   d. 1989

SATA—Vol. 9 pp. 106–108.

3rd Book of Junior Authors—
   pp. 132–133

## 37. One Fine Day by Nonny Hogrogian c.1971

Nonny Hogrogian, the winner of two Caldecott Medals, tells us in SATA Volume 74, "I am always dissatisfied with my work, always left with the feeling that I must try harder the next time." No wonder she has written and illustrated such well-loved books for your children. This Armenian folk tale continues to play well with young audiences because it is one that I shared with my preschool classes, and they all enjoyed it. Perhaps it's because the sly fox must endure quite a bit before the old lady finally sews his beautiful, bushy tale back on. Or perhaps it's the repetition similar to the Mother Goose poem about poor Jack climbing over the stile.

In the beginning the crafty fox helps himself to some milk in a pail, which really belongs to an old lady who is nearby gathering sticks for her fire. She notices the dastardly deed and immediately chops off his tail. She tells him he must give her some milk before she will sew his tail back on. Before the tale is done, the now repentant fox must find grass for the cow, water for the grass, a jug for the water, a blue bead for the fair maiden, and egg for the peddler, and some grain for the hen. In fact, everyone asks for something in return except the kind miller near the end of the story who agrees to give the now "desperate" fox some grain.

In addition to the Caldecott she won for this book, Hogrogian also won the medal in 1966 for "Always Room For One More." Both books are still in print, as I write this.

Birthdate—May 1932

SATA—Vol. 74 pp. 126–130

## 38. Harold and the Purple Crayon Story and pictures by Crockett Johnson c.1955

There are many reasons for the continued popularity of the amiable Harold, with the small size of the book (approximately 4" x 6") and its simplicity being two of its main attributes. However, I believe that it's Harold's control over his immediate environment that makes it so popular with little ones. The pajama-clad Harold and his trusty crayon are invincible, creating, among other things, a mountain, a cityscape boasting millions of windows (my favorite page), and even a picnic replete with all nine kinds of pie that Harold likes best.

The dog-eared, taped up and thoroughly yellowed copy that our family owns is inscribed Thomas Ayer in our lawyer son's first grade scrawl, carefully dated 1976. So you see, the wide-eyed, Harold has been much loved in our family for a long time.

Teachers of young children may want to swathe their room in purple every year on October 20. For you see, the late David Johnson Leisk, whom we knew and loved as Crockett Johnson, was born on this date in 1906 on East 58th Street in N.Y.C. The one-time professional football player married children's writer Ruth Krauss (The Carrot Seed) in 1940 and published this, his first Harold book, fifteen years later when he was 49.

After teachers create their classroom purplescape, they needn't take it down any time soon, since many of the Harold sequels are still available today.

> Birthdate—October 20, 1906 d. 1975
>
> SATA—Vol. 30 pp. 141–144.
>
> 3rd Book of Jr. Authors—pp. 152–153
>
> Books Are By People—pp. 121–124

## 39. Jump, Frog, Jump by Robert Kalan. c.1981.

Every now and then, while teaching preschool, I would come across an almost perfect book for three and four-year olds, that was just right for one of our monthly units. My teaching aide, Mabel Keathley, a book-loving grandmother, introduced me to this one. In March 1991, I was able to purchase a paperback copy from See Saw Book Club, a division of Scholastic. It was just what we needed for our frog unit.

Why is it so good for the preschool set? There are several reasons, with the repetition of the title on every other page throughout the book being the most important one. Little ones love predictable books, probably because they can shout out the simple words during storytime.

Secondly, Byron Barton's self proclaimed "intense colors in flat shapes" are just right for this "house that Jack built" type of story also. The talented Barton is also the illustrator of Bullfrog Builds a House, by Rosamond Dauer, another of my favorites, which is unfortunately now out of print. Do check and see if your library still has it, or search for it at garage sales.

According to his publisher, Greenwillow, now a division of Harper Collins, author Robert Kalan was born in Los Angeles. He has a master's degree in education from Claremont men's College and has taught kindergarten and fourth grade, as well as reading for both gifted and remedial students. Unfortunately, I could find no other biographical information about Kalan in any of my regular sources.

## 40. The Snowy Day   Story and pictures by Ezra Jack Keats c.1962

Young children usually view the first snowfall as a gift from heaven, a free toy, so to speak, while we world-weary adults too often see it as a burden, an inconvenience to our busy lives.

We adults can often learn a lot from children and Peter, the preschool protagonist in this book, is an excellent teacher. Even though he appears to be about four in this book he had been "growing" for quite some time when he began to enter-tain us many years ago. His prototype, a picture taken from an old Life magazine, had hung on the wall of Keats' studio for 22 years, before he debuted to his adoring public in the form of this Caldecott winner.

Brooklyn born Keats, who is white, grew up with chil-dren of all races and felt strongly that African American chil-dren should be portrayed in a more realistic manner in children's books.

Not a single toy from those bewildering toy emporiums appears in this book, yet Peter enjoys himself immensely. He makes all kinds of neat tracks in the soft snow, builds a snow-man and creates a few snow angels. He tells all his adventures to his mother as she gently removes his wet socks and pre-pares a warm bath for him. The next day, he wisely doubles his fun by inviting his friend from across the hall to accom-pany him!

There are lots more books about Peter and his friends and, luckily, many of them are still available.

Birthdate—March 11,1916 d. 1983.

SATA—Vol. 57 pp. 77–87

Junior Book of Authors—p. 120

Books Are By People—pp. 116–120

## 41. The Fat Cat—A Danish Folktale.  Translated and illustrated by Jack Kent c.1971

Quick! Describe the Danish flag for me. If this task is beyond you, perhaps you could check with your four year old, especially if he or she is an avid fan of this book.

The late Jack Kent, who died of leukemia in October 1985, dedicated this perennial favorite to the "Danes in my life," and the fat cat is shown carrying the red flag with a white cross on the dedication page. Born on March 10, 1920 in Burlington, Iowa, Kent was a free-lance artist and internationally know cartoonist for 15 years. He began writing and illustrating children's books full time in 1968, eventually writing more than seventy books.

When our children were young, this tale was another of the books that we read over and over. However, I did hesitate to read it to other people's three and four-year-olds when I starting teaching preschool fearing they might be at least a little bit afraid of the gluttonous feline. No problem—they loved it too!

Living out what has to be the world's worst culinary nightmare, this initially very normal-looking cat manages to consume the following items in a relatively short period of time—some gruel and the pot it was cooked in, and an old woman, portly Skohottentot, svelte Skolinkenlot, five birds in a flock, seven girls dancing, a lady with a pink parasol, and a parson with a crooked staff. He wrongly assumes that he is also going to consume a woodcutter with an axe. As you may have guessed, the woodcutter helps everyone to escape, and to console children, Kent wisely portrays the once again normal-sized cat with a bandage on his tummy on the final page.

Several other books by Kent that your little ones will surely enjoy remain available as of this writing, and if you are really lucky, you may be able to find Why Can't I Fly? By

Ruth Gelman at a garage sale for a quarter or so. Now out of print, it is a very funny story which was illustrated by Kent.

Birthdate—March 10, 1920

SATA—Vols. 24 and 25.

Junior Book of Authors and
   Illustrators—pp. 171–173.

## 42. The Man Who Didn't Wash His Dishes by Phyllis Krasilovsky. c.1950

Although the writing process is normally enhanced for me when the early morning sun is making rainbow patterns through the prisms in my east window, writing this particular review almost necessitated a dreary downpour. For you see, if it hadn't rained near the end of this clever story, the dish-washing crisis might never have been averted.

The nameless hermit in the book is normally quite diligent about washing his dishes immediately after supper. This behavior pattern satisfies him and his small black cat. However, one evening he is especially hungry, and makes himself an extremely large, delicious supper. He is so tired when he finishes eating that he decides to leave his dishes in the sink. Big mistake! Because like all of us, the more he ate, the more he wanted to eat. So every night after finishing larger and larger meals, he is more and more tired and less and less inclined to do his dishes. The crisis continues until he is eating out of ashtrays and flowerpots, having dirtied ALL of his normal dishes.

Luckily, one of the afore-mentioned rainy days comes along just in the nick of time. The clever man piles all of his dirty dishes in the back of his pick-up truck and lets the rain wash them. As you can imagine, he never again lets his daily domestic duties go undone.

Like Kevin Henkes, who also published his first book at 19, Krasilovsky was 19 and newly married when her young husband showed this book to a publisher.

Although it is currently out of print, do look for it at garage sales and used book sales. If you find it you'll not only own a great story, but also one of the first books illustrated by the legendary Barbara Cooney.

Birthdate—August 28, 1926

SATA—Vol. 38 pp. 99–108.

More Junior Authors—pp.
123–126

## 43. The Carrot Seed by Ruth Krauss. c.1945.

Ruth Krauss tells us in SATA Volume 39 that this classic 98 word gem actually "began as a 10,000 word story that was simplified," so comparing the original version to its final form is like comparing a full grown carrot to its tiny seed.

Growing up in Baltimore without television, Krauss also relates that her father read to her from David Copperfield, and her grandfather often read the 23rd psalm to her.

The nameless and nearly faceless little boy in this simple story overcomes parental and older brother skepticism and cares for his carefully planted carrot seed daily by watering it and pulling the surrounding weeds. Ignoring his family, he continues his daily ritual even though "nothing came up." Eventually, his persistence pays off as he harvests a single carrot so huge it requires a wheelbarrow for transportation.

A Hole Is to Dig c. 1952, is another of her many books that I especially like, probably because the "definitions" in the book came from kindergarten children.

The author married children's writer Crockett Johnson, and both were friends of Maurice Sendak, who credits Krauss with helping him launch his writing career.

> Birthdate—July 25, 1911 d. 1993.
>
> SATA—Vol. 30 pp. 143–147.
>
> More Jr. Authors—p. 126.
>
> Books Are By People—pp. 121–124

## 44. The Story of Ferdinand by Munro Leaf. c.1936

When Ferdinand was just a very young bull in Spain, he would never fight and butt heads like the other pasture inhabitants. He would rather "sit quietly and smell the flowers." Too bad the bullfight promoter's didn't see him then, as he lolled peacefully under illustrator Robert Lawson's amusing version of a cork tree. Unfortunately, they happened to see him after he was all grown and attempted to sit under that self-same tree in a particular spot already inhabited by an angry bumblebee. (You'd be mad too if someone as large as Ferdinand tried to sit on you!)

Mistakenly assuming that the "snorting" Ferdinand is a fierce bull, the promoters take him to the bullfights in Madrid whereupon " all the lovely ladies had flowers in their hair." Being the clever person that you are, I am sure you have guessed what Ferdinand did rather than fight the matador that day.

Written in just 25 minutes on a rainy Sunday afternoon, this book was once more popular than Gone With the Wind, according to Jim Trelease in his Read Aloud Handbook.

Leaf, a graduate of Harvard, was also runner up for the Caldecott Medal in 1939 for Wee Gillis.

> Birthdate—December 4, 1905 d. 1976
>
> SATA—Vol. 20 pp. 99–104
>
> Junior Book of Authors—pp. 190–191
>
> Books Are By People—pp. 128–131.

## 45. Frederick  Story and pictures by Leo Lionni c.1967.

S triving to be more organized is an ongoing struggle for me, as I theorize it may be for many creative people.

Frederick, the seemingly unorganized droopy-eyed mouse in this 39 year-old selection, leans toward the ethereal side as well, as he watches his diligent cohorts busily prepare for the up-coming winter days. When they fuss at him for not working, he responds, "I do work, I gather sun rays for the cold winter days." He also collects colors, "for winter is gray." In addition, he stores up words, lest they "run out of things to say."

Naturally, before the long season is over, the mice have not only eaten all the necessary provender in the granary, they have also called upon Frederick to supply the warmth of the sun, the colors of summer and the poetry that feeds our souls.

Lionni, a native of Amsterdam, became a naturalized American citizen in 1945. He has a Ph. D in economics and started writing children's books when he was 49. Frederick, a Caldecott Honor Book, was published when he was 57. He has 23 titles currently listed in Children's Books in Print, and your little ones will surely enjoy them all.

Birthdate—May 5, 1910.

SATA—Vol. 72 pp. 157–162.

3rd Book of Jr. Authors—pp. 179–180.

Books Are By People—pp. 149–151.

## 46. Frog and Toad Together    Story and pictures by Arnold Lobel c.1971

Please don't ever pass up a Lobel book when you are checking out neighborhood garage sales. Although I've read nearly all of the books that he published in his all too brief lifetime, I've never read one that I didn't like, nor have I ever read one to children that was poorly received.

We get the feeling as we read this second book in his popular Frog and Toad series that the two have known each other for a very long time. They are comfortable with each other's foibles, as they stuff themselves with freshly baked cookies and offer advice about such varied topics as gardening and becoming better organized.

There are five brief chapters, and in the fourth one simply titled "Dragons and Giants," the two old friends attempt to determine if they are brave. They take a walk and encounter a "big snake," an avalanche, and a menacing hawk. Then they high tail it home and end up hiding in the bed and closet, respectively, feeling very brave together.

Born in Los Angeles and educated at the Pratt Institute, Lobel commanded 28 pages in Volume 55 of Something About the Author, more than any other author in the series. He felt that he did his best work after 1970, so here are just a few of those still available titles that your four, five or six year old will surely enjoy—Owl At Home (1975), Mouse Soup (1977), A Treeful of Pigs (1979), Ming Lo Moves the Mountain (1982), and Whiskers and Rhymes (1985), and Fables (1980), an amazing book, suitable for all ages.

Birthdate—May 22, 1933 d. 1987.

SATA—Vol. 55 pp. 89–107.

Books Are By People—pp. 156–159.

## 47. Put Me in the Zoo   Story and pictures by Robert Lopshire c.1960.

As my husband and I prepared for our second Christmas together in 1966, I purchased this book and put it under the tree for our unborn oldest daughter. The strategy seems to have paid off, because as most of you know, children who have books in their possessions from birth on tend to love books and reading. Also "readers become writers," and our grown daughter now works for a newspaper.

Lopshire's behavior was slightly unorthodox, too, when he slipped this manuscript in among other writer's offerings when he was employed as a creative art director at Random House. Let's let him tell you what happened, "Banzaii! Put Me in the Zoo was accepted and my silly career was launched as a kiddie-book type. I intended the first and most of the following for people of my own intelligence level-six year-olds."

Lopshire's polka-dotted, four-legged creature wanders into the zoo one day and insists that the zookeepers let him stay. They refuse, and he begins stating his case to the only available on-lookers, a nameless boy and girl. Through forty fantastically colorful pages, he proceeds to demonstrate to them all the things he can do with his spots, such as make them blue, orange and green, juggle with them and make them very small. Awestruck, the children exclaim that he "should NOT be in the zoo."

If your brain does not work like that of a six-year-old, I'm afraid you'll have to find your own copy to determine just where he finally ends up living.

Like many excellent authors, Lopshire takes about a year to write and illustrate a book. He claims to get his best ideas from "politician's speeches, and hour in the bathtub, or a long drive in the car."

Birthdate—April 14, 1927

SATA—Vol. 6, pp. 149–150.

## 48. The Poky Little Puppy by Janette Sebring Lowrey c.1942.

Writers tend to live a long, long time, and Lowery was no exception. Born in Orange, Texas in 1892, the former English teacher was still very much alive in 1986 when she was living in San Antonio and working on a juvenile book and an adult novel. A little quick math will tell you that she was 94 when she did that SATA interview. She died later that year.

When the poky little puppy and his four equally mischievous siblings dig holes under a neighbor's fence, they are reprimanded and denied dessert. The lesson sinks in finally, and they sneak out in the middle of the night to repair the damage. Luckily their mother catches them doing this good deed, and they are rewarded with strawberry shortcake.

Unfortunately for the poky little puppy, he is running late once again, and the dessert is all gone when he finally arrives.

The late Gustaf Tenggren's compelling illustrations, along with the author's careful choice of repeated phrases, "roly-poly, pell-mell, tumble-bumble" have combined to make this one of the largest selling children's books of all time, selling more than 18 million copies to date.

The Poky Little Puppy was one of the twelve original Little Golden Books which sold for a quarter, and it can still be had in many stores for a dollar or two.

Lowrey "fell in love with Dickens" the summer she was twelve. Hmmm, do you suppose if more homes today contained a complete set of Dickens, more of our children might become writers?

> Birthdate—March 2, 1982 d. 1986.
>
> SATA—Vol. 43 pp. 156

## 49. Brown Bear, Brown Bear, What Do You See?
## By Bill Martin, Jr. c.1967.

High quality books for young children which stand the test of time, are categorized in many ways. Here are two concepts that almost always work. First of all, the author can insert humor in a factual story, such as Frank Asch's incomparable Bear Books. Secondly, there are rhythm and rhyme books which little ones love to memorize and hear over and over. Guitar-playing Bill Martin, Jr. is a natural at this poetic style. He has even managed to incorporate Crayola's eight basic colors plus white into this 39 year-old poem.

Who can forget those famous opening lines?

"Brown Bear, Brown Bear, what do you see?"

"I see a redbird looking at me."

Yes, sequels do sometimes take a long time in the publishing world, but we waited 25 years for Polar Bear, Polar Bear, What Do You Hear? Also illustrated by Eric Carle, it was published in 1991, and I like it just as well as Brown Bear.

If preschoolers are a part of your life, you will also want to locate a copy of Chicka, Chicka, Boom Boom c. 1989, another book by Martin, which is also very popular with the younger set.

Martin is another famous author who had a great deal of trouble of learning to read. He finally overcame that obstacle in college, eventually obtaining his Ph.D. in 1961. He was a school principal for six years in Winnetka, Illinois and published this book at the age of 51.

Birthdate—March 20, 1916.

SATA—Vol. 67 pp. 120–125.

## 50. When I Get Bigger   Story and pictures by Mercer Mayer c.1983.

Mercer Mayer who was born in Little Rock, Arkansas, was 40 years old when this book, the second in his "Little Critter" series, was published. It is fairly typical for a children's author to start doing his best work in his 40's or later. There are more than 40 books in Mayer's Little Critter series now, and these inexpensive paperbacks published by Golden Press make excellent additions to your preschoolers library. He told SATA that it is the most popular of all his series, with more than fifty million books in print.

The wide-eyed, beaver-toothed, straw-haired Little Critter in this 203-word book seems fairly complacent about the fact that he is too little to do lots and lots of things that older kids and grownups get to do. For example, he knows that when he gets bigger, he'll be able to go to the corner store by himself, spend his allowance as he chooses and cross the street with the green light. He'll even have his own watch, be able to take the bus to Grandma and Grandpa's and wonder of wonders, go to that magical land known as first grade. He'll have his own paper route and make "lots of money", choose his own boots at the shoe store, and even order something out of the catalog. When the dreamed-about gadget arrives, it's quite a mystery as to what it is, making this one of my favorite pages. Little Critter begins yawning as the book nears its end, and drags his blankie towards his bed, because he knows he can't stay up late, since he is "not bigger yet."

As an artist who was told by an art director in New York to throw away his portfolio because it was so bad, Mayer seems to have established a definite niche in the field of children's literature.

Birthdate—December 30, 1943.

SATA—Vol. 73 pp. 138–144.

4th Book of Junior Authors—
  pp. 259–260.

## 51. Too Much Noise by Ann McGovern c.1967.

Is the phrase "quiet house" an oxymoron? Factor in a young child or two, and it surely is.

Or perhaps it's all relative as Peter, the old hermit in this story finds out. Like Peter, if you've ever spent any time at all in a house by yourself, you know that the sounds it emits can sometimes be scary and annoying.

Peter gets a little tired of hearing the "bed creak," the floor squeak" and the "leaves fall on the roof." So, of course, he consults the wise man of the village who advises, "Get a cow." "What good is a cow?" Peter understandably replies. But ultimately he gets the cow and several other creatures, including a donkey, a sheep, a hen, and finally a dog and a cat. Little ones love repeating all the sounds these animals put forth as they make Peter's tiny home more and more crowded and NOISY.

You guessed it—Peter goes stomping back to the wise man, who calmly advises him to get rid of the animals, one-by-one, whereupon his little cottage becomes very quiet indeed.

Born in New York, Ann McGovern enjoys travel, photography and scuba diving. She was employed by Scholastic as an editor from 1958–1967 and founded the See Saw Book Club for them in 1965. She is also quite well known for her nonfiction titles such as If You Grew Up With Abraham Lincoln (1966) and If You Lived With the Sioux Indians (1974).

Birthdate—May 25, 1930

SATA—Vol. 70 pp. 148–152.

4th Book of Jr. Authors and
    Illustrators—pp. 241–242.

Books Are By People—pp.
    176–178.

## 52. Make Way For Ducklings Story and pictures by Robert McCloskey c.1941.

Are you obsessive enough to be a writer/illustrator? When Robert McCloskey was researching the concept of duck-drawing in preparation for writing this book after spending countless hours sketching mallard ducklings in the Boston Public Gardens, he still wasn't satisfied with his results. So, with no objection from his roommate, illustrator Marc Simont, he began keeping ducks in their apartment!

Based on a true story, as the really good ones often are, this Caldecott winner is the tale (sorry!) of Mr. And Mrs. Mallard and their search for the perfect home in which to raise their impending family. Quite the "shopper" like many of us women, Mrs. Mallard rejects all her husband's suggestions, until they finally choose an island smack dab in the middle of the Charles River near the Public Garden in Boston. (If you've never been to Ben Franklin's lovely old hometown, promise me you'll go someday.)

Michael the policeman feeds them peanuts every day, as do the tourists enjoying the Swan boats.

After Jack, Kack, Lack, Mack, Nack, Ouack, Pack and Quack are safely hatched, old dad takes off for a week, trusting his wife to care for the children. And with the help of the faithful policeman Michael, she does just that, even taking them along on a walk through the busy streets.

Other picture book favorites by the Hamilton, Ohio native include Blueberries For Sal (c. 1948), One Morning in Maine (c.1952) and the 1958 Caldecott winner Time of Wonder.

Married and the father of two adult children Sally and Jane, McCloskey was the first person to ever win the Caldecott twice.

Birthdate—September 15, 1914.

SATA—Vol. 39 pp. 138–148.

Junior Book of Authors—pp. 203–204.

Books Are By People—pp. 164–168.

## 53. Little Bear by Else Holmelund Minarik c.1957.

Little Bear was a commanding presence in our home when our three children were young in the late 60's and early 70's. He was much read and much discussed, since our two oldest couldn't decide which of the four chapters they liked the best. Our oldest daughter was three when we acquired this first book in Harper's "I Can Read" series. As I recall, she preferred the first chapter, "What Will Little Bear Wear?" This was a special favorite, too, every year in February when my preschool class studied "Bears—Because We Love Them." They never failed to see the humor and love in the 11-page chapter as Little Bear constantly interrupts his busy mother to ask for a hat, a coat, and snowpants to counteract the winter chill. She patiently complies with all of these requests until he asks for a "fur coat, too." Mother Bear acquiesces by removing his previously requested garments, and Little Bear happily goes out to play in the snow.

Danish born Minarik trod the path of her celebrated countryman, H.C. Andersen, when she wrote this story for her first grade class on Long Island. Editor Ursula Nordstrom proclaimed "this was just what she had been looking for," and several more Little Bear tales followed. All are charmingly illustrated in the Victorian manner by the versatile Maurice Sendak.

Birthdate—September 12, 1920

Something About the Author—
Vol. 15 pp. 197 & 198.

Third Book of Junior Authors—
pp. 197–198

Books Are By People—pp.
187–190.

## 54. Thomas' Snowsuit   Story and pictures by Robert Munsch c.1985.

It is often said here in Indiana that if you don't like the weather, wait a while and it will change. It is January 12th as I write this, and even though it was too icy for my early morning walk yesterday, it is 58 degrees today!

Our adult son, Tom doesn't like these "wimpy winters" and was a deliriously happy nine-old when the blizzard of "78" swept through the Midwest.

Red-headed Thomas in the story is a lot more reluctant to put on his snowsuit than our Thomas was. In fact, he flatly refuses to put on the new brown garment. Proclaiming it "the ugliest thing I have ever seen in my life." Thomas' mother, like all mothers everywhere, retorts, "We will see about that."

If you have ever tried to put any clothing item on an uncooperative preschooler, you know why few of us needed aerobics classes at that stage of our lives.

An altercation also ensues between the teacher (a truly lovely creature) and the child, with the principal entering the fray as well. Finally, a child yells from the playground for Thomas to come out and play. You guessed it, he "ran across the room, jumped into his snowsuit, got his boots on in about two seconds, and ran out the door."

Canadian Robert Munsch is from a family of nine children. He is a former pre-school teacher who literally tells his stories to hundreds of children before he feels they are good enough to publish. His most well known book, "Love You Forever," should be included in every home library.

Birthdate—June 11, 1945.

SATA—Vol. 50 pp. 153–158.

## 55. Who Took the Farmer's Hat? By Joan L. Nodset. c.1963.

Some books are just simply more fun to read aloud to little ones than others, and this paperback may be the most fun of all because of my very unique and ancient prop that I always don for the presentation. I ask the preschoolers to shut their eyes, then I put on my decrepit straw hat and model it while I read. Talk about an attention getter! Their eyes never leave my face as I read this large print tale, which was originally published by Harper and Row.

As you will see, a windy day early in March when the birds are the busiest, is usually the best time to read it, as well.

The nameless farmer in this brief tale had a favorite hat which was almost as old as he was. He dearly loved it, but one day, the wind whisked it off his head. Chasing after his hat, he begins to question the animals along the way.

Squirrel hasn't seen it, but he did see "a fat round brown bird in the sky." Likewise, the mouse "saw a big round brown mousehole in the grass" and the duck "saw a silly round brown boat", but the bird took that. Now we are getting somewhere, aren't we?

Surely you are clever enough to know what that little red bird needed it for. The kindly farmer subsequently hies himself off to town to purchase a spanking new hat, and everyone is happy.

Illustrator Fritz Siebel was born in Vienna and has worked in television advertising. He is credited with giving birth to Mr. Clean. Information in the back of an early edition of the book also tells us that the author, whose real name is Joan M. Lexau, enjoys photography and gardening along with her writing. She lives in New York state.

Also, be sure to look for her recently reissued "Go Away,

Dog" (1963). It is available in a large print format from Barnes & Noble Publishers for just $5.98.

SATA—Vol. 36 pp. 129–134.

4th Book of Junior Authors— pp. 225–226.

Books Are By People—pp. 144–148.

## 56 If You Give a Mouse a Cookie by Laura Joffe Numeroff c.1985.

Reading this classic book aloud to young children, you might assume that Ms. Numeroff has never worked at any other occupation. You would be wrong about that, since she has also had such varied occupations as running a merry-go-round and working as a private investigator. However, Something About the Author, Volume 142, also tells us that she began writing and illustrating books as a very young child and has a BFA from the famed Pratt Institute, where she graduated with honors.

Numeroff was just 32 years old when she published this award-winning book, which is just as much fun to read aloud to young children now as it was more than 20 years ago when it was first published.

The nameless young boy, sitting on a rock on the first page, is just trying to be kind when he offers one of his cookies to an overall-clad mouse. Little did he know where this gesture might lead. Naturally, the mouse asks for some milk to go with the cookies, which of course requires a straw. Hmmm! Where are the straws? After emptying out an entire small cupboard, the boy finds one. Politely using a napkin, the mouse checks the bathroom mirror to see if he has a milk mustache and decides his hair needs bit of a trim. Cleaning up after himself, he sweeps and scrubs the entire house, making a huge mess and exhausting himself so much that he definitely needs a nap. And everyone knows that can't take a proper nap without hearing a story first. Hearing the story makes him want to draw a picture, which, of course, needs to be taped to the refrigerator. Looking at the refrigerator reminds him that he is thirsty for a glass of milk, and Heaven knows you can't drink a glass of milk without———-a cookie!

This 289 word picture book, with wonderfully coordinated pictures by Felicia Bond, will only take you about 3 minutes to read aloud, but be warned. You will probably have to read it aloud many, many times. There are also several related titles including "If You Give a Pig a Pancake," another of my favorites.

Birthdate—July 14, 1953

SATA—Vol. 142 pp. 141–146

## 57. The Diggingest Dog   Story and pictures by Al Perkins c.1967

If you still don't believe that old axiom that "it's not what you know, it's who you know," perhaps I should tell you that Al Perkins and Ted Geisel were classmates at Dartmouth. After a chance meeting many years later, Geisel (Dr. Seuss) encouraged Perkins to start writing children's books, because he could remember Perkins drawing pictures all over his college notebooks and writing stories about them.

However, I for one feel that the now-deceased, cum-laude graduate would have eventually found his way into the field anyway, because he was the author of our son's favorite book. The summer our son Tom was four, we sat on the front porch in the sun and read this book nearly every afternoon.

When we first meet Duke, he is chained up in a pet shop, "the saddest dog you could ever see." Sammy Brown soon rescues him and takes him home to their farm where Duke learns to dig after several pages of frustration and humiliation. Sad to say though, he learns to dig a bit too well and seemingly can't be stopped. How all this is resolved after 64 pages of excellent rhythm and rhyme makes for a very satisfying ending to this Random House Beginner Book.

Even though our son does not claim to have a favorite part, mine is near the end of the book, when the irrepressible Duke "dug back the garden of Mrs. Thwaites."

Luckily, two of Perkins other older books are now available as board books, so do look for "Hand, Hand, Fingers Thumb" (1969) and The Nose Book (1970). Both currently sell for just $4.99.

Birthdate—August 27, 1904 d. 1975.

SATA—Vol. 30 pp. 168–170.

## 58. The Little Engine That Could by Watty Piper c.1930.

Shattering all your illusions, I am sorry to tell you that Watty Piper is not a real person. According to a Publisher's Weekly article of August 31, 1990, it is simply a name made up by publisher's Platt and Munk in 1930, when an exhaustive six-year search failed to turn up the real author. Their 1930 edition, which was sold for 24 years, was illustrated by Lois Lenski.

The story itself reminds me somewhat of the Biblical "Good Samaritan" story where-in several logical choices to be a "good helper" pass up the unfortunate beggar, with an illogical choice finally giving the necessary aid.

In this classic story, the happy little train puffs and chugs along merrily with her precious cargo of toys and food for the good boys and girls on the other side of the mountain. After an abrupt and unexplained stop, the toys try to flag down several trains to help pull her over the mountain. No less than three ignoble characters (engines) disdain her request and go on about their business, while the little train sits idle. Her Herculean task of pulling the train over the mountain is accomplished mostly because she "thinks she can," an important lesson for all of us as we thread our way through life. The Little Engine That Could has sold more than eight million copies, and the universal appeal for young children is certainly that the hero is a "very little" blue engine.

Although many versions of this book are available, shopping for yours at a train store is always fun.

## 59. The Tale of Peter Rabbit   Story and pictures by Beatrix Potter c.1901.

My good friend Cindy, who lives in Spencer, In., has several acquaintances who are avid proponents of home schooling, and the movement continues to grow in our area as well. Born in 1866, Helen Beatrix Potter and her younger brother, Walter, spent their early years in the third floor nursery of their wealthy Victorian home in London at #2 Bolton Gardens. Educated at home, they also took daily walks and were allowed to keep an extensive menagerie in their combination nursery/school room. Perhaps these two educational aspects warrant a closer look by today's educators also.

The oldest story reviewed in this book, this oft-rejected tale was originally written in the form of a letter to a young five-year-old friend who was ill. The determined 35-year-old Potter self-published the book in time for the Christmas season of 1901, and it was subsequently picked up the following year by Frederick Warne and Company in New York.

Most readers are familiar with the story of the well-behaved girl bunnies Flopsy, Mopsy and Cottontail, and the naughty boy-bunny Peter, but it is important to note that today's three, four, and five-year-olds love the story too. I was surprised and pleased to learn this when I tried it out on my preschool classes a few years ago.

Since there are many, many versions of this tale today, you may want to look for one that has the original text and pictures. The version that I usually read aloud to little ones is a Scholastic paperback illustrated by David McPhail.

Birthdate—July 28, 1866 d.
1943

Junior Book of Authors
pp.247–249

## 60. Curious George Goes to the Hospital   Story and Pictures by Margret and H.A. Rey c.1966.

Every once in a while, a sequel comes along that I like better than the original, and Curious George Goes to the Hospital is a fine example of this phenomenon, in my opinion.

Published exactly 25 years after the original Curious George, this story seems to have a bit more depth, but more importantly it seems to appeal to the four-and five-year-old set more. At 41 pages, it is somewhat longer than most of the books reviewed in this anthology. While it would work well with younger children in a one-on-one situation, I would suggest saving it for the Kindergarten or Pre-Kindergarten groups in a school setting because of the length. Curious George stuffed toys are still available in many bookstores also, and will enhance the story time period as well.

Poor Curious George! His inquisitive mind has landed him in trouble once again, as he inadvertently swallows a piece of the jigsaw puzzle that the man in the yellow hat had intended to give him as a gift.

When his tummy begins to trouble him a bit later on, the man takes him to Dr. Baker who suggests that he go to the hospital for x-rays. Lo and behold, the lost puzzle piece is discovered in his tummy.

George manfully endures many of the hospital procedures that any small child might go through.

However, George, being George, not only comes through the minor surgery successfully, but also cheers up several of the sad young patients, with very unusual disruption of normal hospital routine.

According to an AP article published in 1991, there were seven original Curious George titles which were published by the Reys. "In 1940, they fled the Nazi invasion on bicycles, carrying manuscripts for Curious George and moved to New York," certainly an auspicious beginning for such a timeless and lovely children's classic.

A hardback book, which contains all seven original stories, is now available and would certainly make a fine gift.

> Birthdates—H.A. Rey
> September 16, 1898 d. 1977.
>
> Margret—May, 1906
>
> SATA—Vols 69 and 26.
>
> Junior Book of Authors—pp.
> 255–256.
>
> Books Are By People—pp.
> 230–233.

## 61. Pierre, a Cautionary Tale   Story and pictures by Maurice Sendak c.1962

How many books can you name that are suitable for preschoolers that have five chapters and a prologue? This minute 48-page gem does.

Here is the prologue in its entirety—

> "There once was a boy named Pierre
>
> who only could say, "I don't care!"
>
> Read his story, my friend, for
>
> You'll find at the end that a
>
> Suitable moral lies there."

The pint-sized, blue-suited imp in this tiny tale simply doesn't care and lets us know this as he responds to every parental suggestion, good or bad, with "I don't care!"

His exasperated parents finally leave him alone and head off to town.

As we begin Chapter 3, "a hungry lion paid him a call," and "asked him if he'd like to die." You can guess Pierre's response, of course, as will your listeners. The lion gladly obliges, only to be rewarded (?) with a severe stomachache, which sends him to bed, where Pierre's parents find him upon their return.

I'll not spoil Sendak's clever ending for you, but can assure you that your little ones will learn a lot from this book, which I feel is the best in this well-known author/illustrator's extremely large body of work.

This is one of the four books in Sendak's amazing Nutshell Library. The others are Chicken Soup with Rice, One Was Johnny and Alligators All Around. All are excellent.

Birthdate—June 10, 1928.

SATA—Vol. 27 pp. 181–201.

More Junior Authors—pp. 181–182.

Books Are By People—pp. 250–254

## 62. Green Eggs and Ham    Story and pictures by Dr. Seuss c.1960.

This incorrigible Sam I Am is on the move, and he almost never slows down during the entire 62 pages of this Random House Beginner Book. He relentlessly tries nearly every approach under the sun to encourage his woe-be-gone, pale yellow, fuzzy housemate to try his new culinary masterpiece, green eggs and ham. But will he like them? Not on your life! Not even "with a goat or on a boat" or in eleven other totally unlikely (but always rhyming) scenarios.

Whoa! Wait a minute, has he tried them? As you can imagine, this is a point I always stress when reading to preschool audiences.

Finally on pages 56 and 57, up to his waist in water and totally surrounded by several of Seuss' incomparable creatures, the confused, top-hatted, protagonist tries them. Lo and behold, "Say, I like green eggs and ham!" I usually tell my audience that this is my favorite page, but the last one where he remembers to thank Sam-I-Am is certainly a close second.

Does Dr. Suess still work with today's children? Absolutely! Try it yourself and see if your little one doesn't ask you to read it again!

Understandably, a mountain of words have been written about the late Dr. Seuss whose first manuscript was rejected 29 times and finally printed by one of his Dartmouth College classmates.

Books Are By People by Lee Bennett Hopkins (c. 1969) and unfortunately, long out of print, contains some of the most "human" information that I have found about him and 103 other authors. When Hopkins asked Seuss "What is rhyme?", he replied, "A rhyme is something without which I would be in the dry-cleaning business!"

Birthdate—March 2, 1904.

SATA—Vol. 27 pp. 107–116.

More Junior Authors—pp. 182–183.

Books Are By People—pp. 255–258.

## 63. Caps For Sale   Retold and Illustrated by Esphyr Slobodkina. c.1940.

S ATA Vol. 1 tells us that Esphyr Slobodkina (slow-boat-keena) was born in Siberia and that she painted trays and wastepaper baskets in New York during the Depression.

I am glad she did, and you should be, too. Perhaps those early, relatively, mundane, and repetitive tasks provided her background images of this "Tale of a Peddler, Some Monkeys and Their Monkey Business" as she subtitles this famous tale.

Using such words as "wares" and "refreshed", the Russian-born author underscores the fact that she doesn't "write down to children."

In fact, the very "cleverness" of this tale seems to be its strongest point when I read it to groups of four-and five-year olds. Boys especially seem to enjoy it.

You see the hard working, self employed peddler in this tale is quite content with his lot in life, strolling from town to town with his chapeaux stored atop his head, selling them to one and all for "fifty cents a cap."

Becoming a little weary one day, he takes a rather lengthy nap beneath a large tree, only to find upon awakening that his caps were missing.

It seems a lively troop of monkeys in the tree is wearing them. When they don't respond to verbal directions to give them back, the peddler throws down his own hat in disgust. A-hah! Guess what happened?

> Birthdate—1909
>
> SATA—Vol.1 p. 210.
>
> 3rd Book of Junior Authors—
>     pp. 268–270.

## 64. Doctor De Soto   Story and pictures by William Steig c.1982

If Dr. De Soto were your dentist, you would enjoy your visits more. You see, even though he is a mouse he does "very good work" and has no end of patients. His wife is his special assistant, and small animals such as chipmunks get to sit in the regular chair. However, as we can see on the very first page, he will also willingly climb a ladder to work on larger animals like the pig all decked out in her pink and purple dress.

The only animals he refuses to work on—-and this was clearly spelled out on his sign—-were "cats and other dangerous animals." This, of course, rules out foxes even though one was in such dire pain outside the office one day that he begged Dr. De Soto to help him. His wise wife urges him to ignore the fox's sob story, since working inside a fox's mouth would surely put his life in peril.

As clever as he is skilled, Dr. De Soto devises a way to outsmart the scoundrel, who plans to eat the dentist once his brand new tooth is in place.

Check this well-loved book out of the library or buy it in the paper back version to read to your child to see who wins this war of wits.

Steig, who has won both the Newbery and the Caldecott, has several other books still in print, but this is one of my favorites to read aloud to young children.

Birthdate—November 14, 1907.

SATA—Vol. 70. pp. 213–218

## 65. The Monster at the End of This Book   Story and pictures by Jon Stone c.1971.

Nearly all of the books in this anthology are fun to read aloud to a group of preschoolers, but this Little Golden Book may be the most fun of all.

Although it seems to flit in and out of print fairly often, I find it rather regularly at antique stores for a dollar or two, and it is sometimes on the racks at drug stores or grocery stores for about the same price. Don't ever pass it up, because you will need extra copies, as your children will love it to death. Of course, it also makes a perfect baby gift, or special something for an older child when a new baby arrives.

The intrepid blue monster named in the title is our friend, lovable, furry old Grover from Sesame Street. Not that he knows he is the monster as we begin the book, because he, Grover-like, is afraid of monsters. He tries his best to make sure you won't turn the pages and get to the end of the book, where that scarry, scarry monster resides. You, the reader, keep turning the pages anyway, even though he, Grover, progressively ties them shut, boards them up ands even builds a brick wall to keep you from turning the pages! He tells you that you are very strong as you keep turning the pages anyway, and naturally he must also shout at you, YOU TURNED ANOTHER PAGE! This is the best part of all for little ones as they "help" you read it aloud.

The recipient of eighteen Emmys over the course of his career, Stone was one of the originators of Sesame Street along with Jim Henson and Joe Raposo. Stone also created Big Bird and the Cookie Monster. In spite of these accomplishments, those of us who are lucky enough to be parents and anyone who has ever worked with small children, should be eternally grateful that he also took the time to write this very clever children's book.

Thus far, the book has sold over five million copies, and Stone told SATA that he wrote it on a plane between New York and Denver, although it was an idea that had been "floating around my head."

Birthdate—April 13, 1931. d. 1997.

SATA—Vol. 39 pp. 199–209.

## 66. The Mitten by Alvin Tresselt. c.1964.

Many of the classic tales reviewed in this book are based on even older folk tales. The title page on this one tells us that it is based on an old Ukrainian folktale and is adapted from the version written by E. Rachev. The copy I have is a Scholastic paperback which is a Blue Ribbon Book, and I've never been disappointed in the story line of any of these books.

Even though it is "the coldest day of the winter" as the story opens, a young boy is gathering firewood for his grandmother. As he returns home, he drops his mitten in the snow, and a tiny mouse adopts it as her home. Feeling generous, she lets a frog and owl join her, although she admits that the latter makes her a little "nervous." Presently a rabbit squeezes in too, and a fox soon requests and receives lodging (It is usually at this point when I asked my pre-school audience which of these animals could actually fit into the mitten).

Soon a big gray wolf and a wild boar "squinch" themselves in, and (can you believe it?) a bear squeezes himself in too "without so much as a please or thank you."

What finally burst the mitten? A tiny black cricket, proving once again that it's the little things in our lives that cause us the most consternation.

Tresselt is also the author of White Snow, Bright Snow, which won the Caldecott Medal in 1948 and many other excellent books for children.

Birthdate—September 10, 1916.

Books Are By People—pp. 286–288.

SATA—Vol. 7 pp. 197–198.

More Junior Authors— pp.211–212.

## 67. A Tree Is Nice by Janice May Udry c.1956.

Artist Marc Simont won the Caldecott Medal for his watercolor pictures in this lovely, mild-mannered book. It is exactly 50 years old as I write this, and it's message is certainly more important today than it was then. I don't think that the term "urban sprawl" existed in those days, and many of us lived on farms with acres and acres of corn and lots of lovely woods where we climbed trees and played countless hours in the shade among the wildflowers. A river ran through our property, too, and decades old Wisconsin weeping willows flourished along its banks.

Perhaps, just perhaps, if every parent of this country's 18 million plus preschoolers would share this book with his or her little one, we might be able to recapture just a bit of that peaceful "green and growing" environment. Even if your little corner of the world consists of just the usual quarter acre lot, you can use this book as your guide to making it a little more friendly for birds, wildlife and TREES!

Udry doesn't tell us exactly how to plant our own tree until the last few pages, but she uses her earlier 300 plus words to tell us just why we should love them. For example, they "fill up the sky" and "make everything beautiful". "Leaves whisper in the breeze all summer long", and when they come down in the fall, we can rake them and make playhouses out of them. A tree makes shade for cows and houses and picnics, too.

A friend of mine, whose husband is a forester, once told me that you can plant a tree during any season of the year, even though fall is the best time. So go purchase a small tree of your own right now, and grab your little one, and go plant it together in your very own yard. Be sure to water it and take very good care of it, as Udry suggests, and it will reward you for many years to come.

Not long ago, I found a hardback copy of Udry's "The Moon Jumpers" (1959) at a library book sale for 30 cents. It is another excellent picture book for little ones. If you have older children (second grade or so), you'll also want to track down "What Mary Jo Shared" (1966).

Birthdate—June 14, 1928

SATA—Vol. 152 pp. 239–240

"Books Are By People" by Lee
Bennett Hopkins. c. 1969.

## 68. Alexander, Who Used to Be Rich Last Sunday by Judith Viorst c.1978.

Chances are pretty good if you are reading this book, you have young children and perhaps even one or two in elementary school or older. If that is true, chances are also excellent that you rarely have any money. Articles about how to manage your money are constantly being printed in women's magazine, and this might be helpful to you, or better yet, just wait until your kids grow up.

This annoying "empty pockets syndrome" is a fact of life for Alexander. The book is also my favorite among the many books that this talented author has written, based on the antics of her three sons.

Being the youngest of three boys is tough enough on Alexander, but when that is coupled with the fact that he is the only one of the three who simply cannot save any money, his dilemma compounds.

He would really like to get a walkie-talkie, and his mom encourages him to save the dollar his grandparents have given him. "Saving money is hard," Alexander laments, wise beyond his years.

Spending just a little of his cache, he purchases a bit of bubble gum and then rents his friend Eddie's snake for an hour. Other well-thought-out purchases include a one-eyed bear and a melted candle at a garage sale, and pretty soon all he has left is "bus tokens."

You may want to purchase Viorst's The Tenth Good Thing About Barney (c.1971) for friends or relatives who have lost family members and are having a hard time explaining it to little ones.

Birthdate—February 2, 1931

SATA—Vol. 123 pp. 171–179

## 69. Owl Babies by Martin Waddell c.1975.

"Read to your children" admonishes a page from an out-dated calendar based upon "Life's Little Instruction Book" by H. Jackson Brown. I've kept that page on my bulletin board for two reasons, even though the calendar itself is long gone. First of all, the date chosen for this succinct bit of wisdom was my dad's birthday March 10. Secondly it is something that every single parent regardless of their circumstances can do for their young child. Even if money is tight at your house, as it is in many households with young children, nearly every public library has programs for babies and toddlers these days. Be sure to sign your children up and then take a few classic books home with you to be enjoyed during the week.

Owl Babies is one of the board books that you may find, in fact, if you are lucky. Reading it to your restless toddler every night will probably help a great deal in calming your little one down.

Owl Babies Sarah, Percy and Bill enjoy a comfortable, predictable life in their hole in the trunk of a tree with their Owl Mother. That is until they awake one night and Owl Mother is GONE! Sarah and Percy, being a bit older, have various expressions they use such as "Oh my goodness" and "Where's Mommy?" as they await Mother's return, but all little Bill can say is "I want my mommy!" As the baby owls wait and think ("All owls think a lot") various things go through their minds, but they are pretty sure she has gone off for food and will soon be back. Finally they decide to comfort themselves by all sitting together on Sarah's branch. Naturally Mother Owl returns about this time and wonders why they were all so concerned.

Waddell has written more than 100 books for children, and my other favorites "Farmer Duck" and "Can't You Sleep, Little Bear?" are both available as board books as well.

Birthdate—April 10, 1944.

SATA—Vol. 127 pp. 217–226.

## 70. The Napping House by Audrey Wood. c.1984.

Nestled between two ancient, gnarled trees, the Napping House appears to be slumbering itself as a gentle rain touches its flower-bedecked yard and white picket fence. Muted blues, greens and purples set the mood as we turn the page to find a contented granny snoring in her slightly rickety, antique bed.

If you're lucky enough to share this classic with a sharp-eyed four or five year old, he or she will probably point out that although Granny definitely appears to be alone in the room, she most certainly is not. Your listener may just be able to find a boy, a dog, a cat, a mouse and even a flea in that first scene, all of whom eventually end up snoozing atop Granny. They pile on Granny in that exact order too, which becomes the key issue near the end of the book when the "wakeful flea" bites the "slumbering mouse" and upsets the entire peaceful pile. No matter. The sun is beginning to peek in the window, the rain has ceased, and it's definitely time for the non-traditional family to begin enjoying the day and each other's company.

Husband and wife Don and Audrey Wood have few equals when it comes to pairing words and pictures in children's picture books. They have many books in print, and your children will love them all. Little Piggies, published in 1991, seems to always tickle young children also.

Audrey Wood is a fourth generation artist whose father also worked for the Ringling Brothers Circus in Florida, where the fat lady and other employees often babysat for her. The Woods have an adult son and currently reside in Santa Barbara, California.

Birthdate—1948

SATA—Vol. 81 pp. 217–222

6th Book of Authors and
　　Illustrators—pp. 320 & 321

## 71. Harry the Dirty Dog by Gene Zion. c.1956.

If you don't know that "boys like dirt" as our son once indignantly informed me, then you must have only daughters peopling your house.

Most small boys do like dirt, and although there are many reasons for the popularity of this classic book, that is probably the main reason why it has endured for so long. For you see the little terrier who is white with black spots detests baths so much that he hides the scrub brush in the back yard and runs away before the children can inflict this periodic torture on him. Then he proceeds to get as dirty as he possibly can by playing "where they were fixing the street," at the railroad, in a dirt pile with his dog friends and getting "dirtiest of all" by sliding down a coal chute. Now he is no longer "a white dog with black spots," but a "black dog with white spots."

Realizing he is in a serious pickle, he, of course, heads back home. Even when he performs all of his tricks in the back yard for his family, they still don't recognize him. Inspiration strikes as he digs up the scrub brush, whereupon he dashes upstairs to the bathroom. As the children begin scrubbing, their beloved Harry, the white dog with black spots, emerges once again. Like nearly all great books for little ones, a humorous twist is added at the end as Harry happily falls asleep on his pillow with the dreaded scrub brush hidden beneath it.

Eugene Zion was born in New York, but his family moved to his neighboring state of New Jersey where he grew up in the rural area of Ridgefield. SATA Vol. 18 also tells us that he loved to read as a child and earned his first money painting designs on the back of the yellow slickers of his school friends. He graduated from the Pratt Institute in New York and married Margaret Bloy Graham, whose book Be

Nice To Spiders, is also in this anthology.

Birthdate—1913 d. 1975.

SATA—Vol. 18 pp. 305–306.

## 72. No Roses For Harry by Gene Zion. c.1958.

Although my research has never substantiated this, it would be my guess that Zion and his wife, author/illustrator Margaret Bloy Graham had a small black and white terrier for a pet. Marjorie Flack had a black terrier when she wrote her timeless Angus stories, and generally only first hand pet experience can produce such high quality, endearing animal stories. Zion and his wife were childless, as well, perhaps adding to the "humanness" of the indomitable Harry.

There are four "Harry" books all together and each one is a treasure. In this second book, Harry is indeed treated like a person as he receives a birthday sweater from Grandma. Unfortunately, it is green with gold roses on it, and the family insists that he wear it. Harry detests it. When the family goes into town to shop the next day, people and dogs alike ridicule his attire. Making up his mind to ditch the sweater, he leaves it behind in different locations, only to have people return it to him. What to do? Moping, he retreats to the back yard, where he discovers a loose thread on the hand knit sweater. Eureka! It begins to quickly unravel as he continues to pull. An industrious bird spots the loose thread and immediately takes it up in a nearby tree where she begins weaving it into a nest. Naturally the nest turns out to be green with gold roses as the family learns after Harry leads them to it. Grandma dutifully replaces the garment at Christmas time, but thankfully this time its white with black spots just like Harry!

Zion's first book All Falling Down (1951) was runner-up for the Caldecott. Like all of his books, it was illustrated by his wife. In addition to Harry, the Dirty Dog, the other two Harry books are Harry and the Lady Next Door (1960)(definitely a favorite at our house) and Harry by the Sea (1965).

In his autobiographical sketch for More Junior Authors

(1963), Zion's last sentence is "No creative effort has been more gratifying for me than writing picture books for children."

Birthdate—1913 d. 1975.

SATA—Vol. 18. pp. 305–306.

## 73. I Like To Be Little by Charlotte Zolotow. c.1987.

It is apropos that Charlotte Zolotow should be the very last author reviewed in this book. Her first book was published more than 50 years ago, and she has written some of the best books in the industry. During the many years that I wrote my newspaper column in Terre Haute, I probably reviewed more books by her that any other author. Even one of her earliest books, The Storm Book is a Caldecott Honor Book and is still available today.

An earlier edition of I Like To Be Little with pictures by Tony de Luna was published as I Want To Be Little in 1966, but I am partial to this Harper Trophy paperback, which I found for just $3.95 in a fine old bookstore in Boston several years ago. The illustrations by my favorite children's illustrator, Eric Blegvad, caught my eye and compelled me to purchase it.

Perhaps the very best thing about this book is that it "celebrates" being little. (Do other cultures push their children to grow up as much as we Americans? I think not.) After all, do we grown-ups "sit under the dining room table, draw with crayons or jump in a pile of leaves each fall?" Certainly not, although perhaps we should take time to do those things with our children. In a thoughtful conversation with her mother, the nameless young girl in this story calmly explains to her mother why she is enjoying being little for now and is in no hurry to grow up.

Lately when a young friend or relative has a baby I give them three paperbacks—-Happy Birthday, Moon, Play With Me, and this very special book.

Zolotow still has several books listed in Children's Books In Print, and many are award winners.

Birthdate—June 26, 1915

SATA—Vol. 78 pp. 258–263.

## 74. Mr. Rabbit and the Lovely Present by Charlotte Zolotow. c.1962.

It seems to be the trend in the decorating world today to choose a certain palette of colors for your home, and even newlyweds are climbing aboard, with only certain colors being permitted for wedding towels, etc. When people ask me what colors we use in our home, I usually respond "pretty colors" or "all colors."

Like the little girl's mother in this Caldecott Honor book, I, too like red, yellow, green and blue. What comes in those colors? Why roofs, caterpillars and lakes, not to mention cardinals, canaries, parrots and bluebirds. However, the little girl in this story is perplexed about a birthday present for her mother and, none of these ideas seems quite suitable.

The helpful rabbit in the story suggests other things too, such as red underwear (always good for a laugh with young audiences) butter, emeralds, and the stars, but these items must be rejected as well, for obvious reasons.

What to do? The rabbit's thinking cap shifts into high gear as he suggests fruit items in the corresponding colors. Apples, bananas, pears and grapes are finally settled upon as a "lovely present," and a basket to put them in is soon produced.

In SATA Vol. 75, Zolotow credits Ursula Nordstrom at Harper Collins for helping her get started as a children's writer. While working as Nordstrom's editorial assistant, she showed her an outline for a book idea. Nordstrom suggested that she add more detail and The Park Book, illustrated by H.A. Rey, was published in 1944.

Birthdate—June 26, 1915

SATA—Vol. 78 pp. 258–273.

## 75. William's Doll by Charlotte Zolotow. c. 1972.

Are involved fathers waxing or waning in your neighborhood? My casual observations at the grocery store and elsewhere tell me that more and more fathers are learning that time spent with their children is much more important than purchasing piles of toys for them.

Quite a few of these young fathers attempt to extract opinions from their tots as well. Charlotte Zolotow would be pleased about this because she tells us in Books Are By People by Lee Bennett Hopkins that "adults...don't respect children enough."

In this story, William's dad is not stingy with gifts, giving him a basketball complete with a goal, and a train set which they play with "a lot." However, he isn't quite in tune with his preschool son's needs as he purchases these typical "boy" gifts.

When William expresses the desire for a baby doll with eyes that open and close, his older brother dismisses the idea as "creepy," and the boy next door says he is a "sissy."

As sometimes happens in real life, William's grandmother is the only one who really listens, and she alone understands that he needs the doll so he can "practice being a father."

Soft illustrations by the late award-winning William Pene du Bois complement this Harper Trophy Paperback, which was also named as a Caldecott Honor Book.

Zolotow's name on any book will assure you of an excellent story, so do look for them at garage sales and antique stores too. Many of her titles can still be ordered in paperback as well.

Birthdate—June 26, 1915.

SATA—Vol. 78 pp. 258–263.

Here are 25 other books your little one will enjoy.

1.  Alborough, Jez —Where's My Teddy? c.1992.
2.  Anglund, Joan Walsh—A Friend Is Someone Who Likes You c.1987.
3.  Ehlert, Lois—Snowballs c.1995.
4.  Fox, Mem—Time For Bed c.1993.
5.  Ginsburg, Mirra—Good Morning, Chick c.1980
6.  Henkes, Kevin—The Biggest Boy c. 1995.
7.  Hill, Eric—Where's Spot? c.1980.
8.  Hoberman, Mary Ann—A House Is a House For Me c.1978.
9.  Hutchins, Pat—Rosie's Walk c.1968.
10. Kellogg, Steven—Can I Keep Him? c.1971.
11. Kasza, Keiko—A Mother For Choco c.1992.
12. Keats, Ezra Jack—Peter's Chair c.1967.
13. Keller, Holly—Geraldine's Big Snow c.1988.
14. Kunhardt, Dorothy—Pat The Bunny c.1940.
15. Lenski, Lois—Cowboy Small c.1949.
16. Lester, Helen—Tacky the Penguin c.1988.
17. Martin, Bill Jr. and Archambault, John—Chicka, Chicka, Boom Boom c.1989.
18. McPhail, David—Emma's Pet c.1985.
19. Rathmann, Peggy—Good Night, Gorilla c.1994.
20. Scarry , Richard—Richard Scarry's Best Word Book Ever c.1980.
21. Sis, Peter—Fire Truck c.1998.
22. Small, David—Imogene's Antlers c.1985.
23. Tafuri, Nancy—Have You Seen My Duckling? c.1984.

24. Wells, Rosemary—McDuff Comes Home c.1997.
25. Williams, Vera B.—More, More, More said the Baby c.1990.

# Acknowledgments—

Special thanks to—

My writer friends Bette Killion and Peggy Cobb for their many years of encouragement.

Lots and lots of strangers who became friends through our mutual love of children's books during my many years of writing my newspaper column in Terre Haute. Thanks especially to Rita Schroeder, Gretchen Van Pelt, Lila Thomas, Todd Nation and retired Indiana State University professor, Dr. William McCarthy.

The lovely Library Ladies in the Young People's section at the Vigo County Public Library in Terre Haute for all the help and support they have given me over the years and continue to give me today. Their knowledge and love of children's books is amazing.

Jacqueline Briggs Martin, children's book author and my outstanding instructor at the University of Iowa Summer Writing Festival during two lovely summer weekend workshops in Iowa City.

Mike Heaton for technical assistance in the final stages of the book.

And finally thanks especially to our book-loving family-our daughters, Tammy and Teresa, our son Tom and his wife Brigid and their three little ones Mary, Joseph and Brigid Grace.

My "computer guy", my husband Gordon deserves the most thanks however, because I do all of my writing on yellow legal pads with my "Jesus Loves the Little Children" pencils, and he does virtually all of my computer work. Thanks, Honey!

# Bibliography

Frank, Josette—Your Child's Reading Today—Doubleday & Co. c. 1969.

Hearne, Betsy—Choosing Books For Children—Delacourt Press c. 1981.

Hopkins, Lee Bennett—Books Are By People—Scholastic c. 1969.

Junior Book of Authors—A series of reference books that contains biographies of children's authors.

Kimmel, Margaret Mary and Segal, Elizabeth—For Reading Out Loud—Delacourt Press c. 1988.

Larrick, Nancy—A Parent's Guide to Children's Reading—Bantam Books c. 1982.

Lipson, Eden Ross—The New York Times Parent's Guide to the Best Books For Children—Three Rivers Press c. 2000.

Silvey, Anita—100 Best Books for Children—Houghton Miflin c. 2004.

Something About the Author—A series of more than 140 reference books which contains biographical information about writers and illustrators of children's books.

Trelease, Jim—The New Read-Aloud Handbook—Penguin Books c. 1989.